100 Strategies to Support Children's Behaviour and Emotional Wellbeing is accompanied by a number of printable online materials, designed to ensure this resource best supports your professional needs.

Go to https://resourcecentre.routledge.com/speechmark and click on the cover of this book.

Answer the question prompt using your copy of the book to gain access to the online content.

T0383624

100 Strategies to Support Children's Behaviour and Emotional Wellbeing

Children's mental health and emotional wellbeing are fundamental to their success in school and in later life. Full of practical ideas and insights, this interactive guide is designed to empower staff to make a difference to children's wellbeing and behaviour by using simple and effective strategies that can easily be implemented throughout the school day.

Taking staff on a journey through the school year, the book identifies issues that are relevant to children at certain times of the year, along with practical strategies to address those challenges. Each half term includes space for self-reflection and notes, with key questions to encourage practice evaluation. Based on the author's extensive experience and conversations with staff working in primary schools, this book:

- Provides school staff with an easy-to-use, accessible resource that promotes their understanding of children's emotional wellbeing and behaviour.

- Introduces reflective language, which is fast, effective and easy to implement with proven results in developing better understanding of children's wellbeing and increasing children's emotional vocabulary in schools.

- Explores the impact of a child's home life on their behaviour in school.

- Encourages staff to build up a personalised pool of resources to refer back to and use.

- Includes ideas for building insight into each child and collecting evidence of strategies which help with Education and Health Care Plans, review meetings, pupil progress and behaviour monitoring meetings with parents/other school staff.

Developing staff understanding and confidence in responding to and meeting children's emotional and mental health needs, this invaluable guide will equip teaching assistants, teachers, special educational needs coordinators (SENCOs) and senior staff to support children in school and empower them to make a difference to children's wellbeing and behaviour.

Cath Hunter is a therapeutic consultant, trainer, play therapist and author with over 40 years' experience of working with children and families. She has provided services to primary schools since 2004, including working with school staff to provide strategies and support for children's emotional wellbeing and behaviour.

'The strategies in this book are practical and help staff respond in a more appropriate way. Over time the strategies become part of normal classroom practice which helps staff develop an environment of mutual respect where children feel safe and are able to express feelings in a more appropriate way' – **Headteacher**

'I would recommend this book to anyone working with children. It changed the way I approached children, enabling me to be more focused on their emotional needs' – **Teaching Assistant**

'Using this guide has changed my everyday practice. I am now more able to see the child instead of the behaviour' – **SENCO**

'Using reflective language had an immediate and positive impact on my relationships with the children' – **Year 4 Teacher**

100 Strategies to Support Children's Behaviour and Emotional Wellbeing

A Practical Toolkit for the School Year

Cath Hunter

Routledge
Taylor & Francis Group

LONDON AND NEW YORK

Designed cover image: Cath Hunter and Jane O'Neill

First published 2024
by Routledge
4 Park Square, Milton Park, Abingdon, Oxon OX14 4RN

and by Routledge
605 Third Avenue, New York, NY 10158

Routledge is an imprint of the Taylor & Francis Group, an informa business

British Library Cataloguing-in-Publication Data
A catalogue record for this book is available from the British Library

Library of Congress Cataloging-in-Publication Data
Names: Hunter, Cath, author.
Title: 100 strategies to support children's behaviour and emotional wellbeing : a practical toolkit for the school year / Cath Hunter.
Other titles: One hundred strategies to support children's behaviour and emotional wellbeing
Description: Abingdon, Oxon ; New York, NY : Routledge, 2024. | Includes index. | Summary
-- Provided by publisher.
Identifiers: LCCN 2023011110 (print) | LCCN 2023011111 (ebook) | ISBN 9781032460246 (hardback) | ISBN 9781032460239 (paperback) | ISBN 9781003379751 (ebook)
Subjects: LCSH: School children--Mental health. | Behavior modification. | Reflective learning. | Emotional intelligence. | Classroom management.
Classification: LCC LB3430 .H88 2024 (print) | LCC LB3430 (ebook) | DDC 371.7/13--dc23/eng/20230502
LC record available at https://lccn.loc.gov/2023011110
LC ebook record available at https://lccn.loc.gov/2023011111

ISBN: 9781032460246 (hbk)
ISBN: 9781032460239 (pbk)
ISBN: 9781003379751 (ebk)

DOI: 10.4324/9781003379751

Typeset in DIN Pro
by Deanta Global Publishing Services, Chennai, India

Access the Support Material https://resourcecentre.routledge.com/speechmark

For Jane

Contents

About this book

This book is the result of hundreds of conversations over many years with teaching assistants, teachers, SENCOs and senior staff who are looking for ways to support children who are unsettled, not fully engaged in learning or whose behaviour is causing concern. I spend much of my week in one-to-one conversations and group training with staff who are passionate about helping the children with whom they work but are also stretched for time. Many of these conversations involve discussing possible reasons for children's behaviour and identifying how to support them.

I encourage staff to reflect on a child's behaviour and to be curious (not always easy) about what the child is doing, what is happening and why they may be behaving in a particular way. I also encourage school staff to explore what may be going on for them, what are they feeling and what are they bringing to the situation. This increased level of self-awareness can be invaluable when dealing with any child, but especially when confronted by challenging behaviour.

I have been very privileged to work alongside some incredible school staff who do a phenomenal job taking care of children on a regular basis. I encounter many school staff who at times feel overwhelmed by the emotional, behavioural and mental health needs of the children they are working with.

Over the years I have developed many strategies that are easy to implement, including the concept of reflective language. This involves using simple statements that enable a child to feel seen and heard, therefore having a powerful impact on their behaviour. This book introduces reflective language and many other strategies that have proved to be very effective in schools.

The book is for individuals who wish to develop their practice in this area, but it is also very appropriate for school teams who wish to evidence their work for EHC applications/plans and review meetings, pupil progress and behaviour monitoring meetings with parents/other school staff. This book can be used as part of a whole-school approach to supporting emotional well-being and behaviour by ensuring a consistent and cohesive approach across the staff team.

Cath Hunter
Therapeutic Family Interventions www.therapeuticfamilyinterventions.co.uk

Cath Hunter is a therapeutic consultant, trainer, play therapist and author with 40 years' experience of working with children and families. She has delivered services to primary schools since 2004.

Introduction

The aim of this book is to increase your awareness and understanding of what motivates children and how to support children's behaviour and learning. It does this by encouraging you to notice and be curious about the behaviours you see in school and by suggesting new strategies for you to try. Children's behaviour is their way of communicating, and as our understanding of what these behaviours mean increases, we become more confident responding to it. By increasing our awareness and thinking about the possible reasons behind a child's behaviour, we are able to develop a deeper understanding of behaviour and emotional wellbeing. This increased awareness may lead to us responding differently, resulting in positive changes in children's behaviour.

When we focus on and notice what a child is trying to tell us by their behaviour, we are able to respond to and meet that need, resulting in the child feeling seen and understood. This boosts our confidence as school staff, resulting in a more positive working environment for ourselves and the children whom we are working with.

Children are expected to manage a great deal during their school lives, including:

- Separating from their parents or carers
- Building and maintaining relationships with other children
- Managing their feelings
- Having resilience to manage getting things wrong
- Constantly trying new things
- Restarting relationships after being told off
- Managing change

How many children in school have the skills to be able to manage all this? Imagine every time you made a mistake all your colleagues knew about it. Imagine every time you went into the staff room, everything on the notice board had been changed around or moved. Imagine being asked to get on with something you don't know how to do. Although situations like this may happen in school, as adults you are able to talk about it and ask for support if you need it.

DOI: 10.4324/9781003379751-1

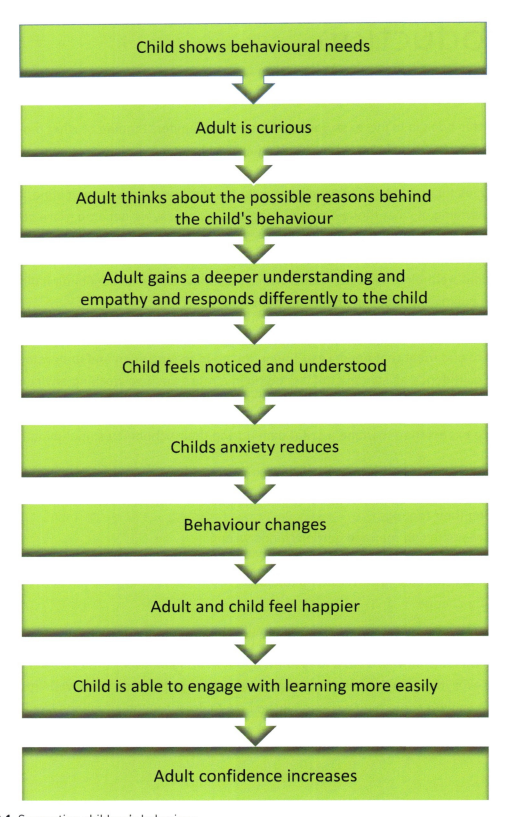

Figure 0.1 Supporting children's behaviour

This book will enable you to experiment with different ways of responding to children's behaviour and try different strategies, along with reflecting on what worked and what didn't and how you feel. This reflective aspect is an important part of the process as it will enable you to identify the changes that occur on a weekly basis.

The book begins by introducing the concept of reflective language, a tool that you are encouraged to experiment with throughout this year.

The book is divided into the six half terms that make up the school year, with each half term focusing on a different theme. Each section will provide an overview of the theme, identifying what the focus is and why. It will describe some of the behaviours you may see and signs to look for, along with exploring some of the possible reasons for the child's behaviour. It encourages you to focus on a different child each week, enabling you to develop a deeper insight into them and to perhaps notice behavioural responses you may not otherwise see. You may also choose to focus on a child for several weeks or the whole half term.

Each section also includes several strategies for you to implement with the child for the week, to support behavioural changes occurring. When using the profile checklist, you may find that only some rather than all of the behaviours apply to a child. If this is the case, I suggest you try some of the strategies and see if they have an impact. It is necessary to be aware that children who are neurodivergent may have different needs and therefore respond differently to some of the strategies I suggest. However, the main focus of this book is about understanding and responding to the individual needs of the child. By using the suggested strategies, you will gain a deeper understanding of the child and be better able to support them.

Each half term begins and ends with a reflection sheet. I encourage you to use this space in the way that suits you. You can write as little or as much as you choose. Experiment with using the book in the way that works best for you. Do it daily, weekly, on your own or with a colleague. There is no right or wrong way of using this tool but I hope that, when looking back over the weeks and half terms, you will notice how things have changed in a positive way.

Throughout the book, for ease, I refer to 'teacher' and 'class', but these strategies are relevant to all school staff, no matter what role you have in school. I encourage you to use this book as a way of developing and improving your relationships with the children you are working with and to enable you to have a more fulfilling relationship with them.

Wishing you an enjoyable year.

What is this child trying to tell me?

Imagine you are a teacher in Year 2 and you had an argument with your partner before you left for work this morning, resulting in you arriving at school late and unprepared. How easy would you find it to settle in at work and perform well? What would you be thinking and feeling? What could you do about this? How could you communicate your feelings and get support? Now imagine you are seven years old and you had an argument with your mum before you left for school this morning, resulting in you arriving late to school without your homework. How easy would you find it to settle into class and engage with your learning? What would you be thinking and feeling? What could you do about this? How could you communicate your feelings and get support?

As adults, we are able to use language to talk about our thoughts and feelings, if we choose to, and can ask for support. We are able to rationalise experiences, know that we will survive them and have the benefit of life experiences to know that things usually pass and life doesn't stay challenging forever. How difficult are any of these for a seven-year-old? It is therefore not surprising that children communicate their feelings and need for support through their behaviour. Children do not want negative comments or attention for challenging behaviour, but some children may have learnt that any attention is better than no attention and therefore may evoke negative reactions from adults. Children who seek attention in the form of disapproval may be showing us they have low self-esteem and may believe that other people are unable to see the good in them. When children are happy and settled, they do not need to ensure that adults remember them; if a child does this, it is an indication that they need additional help and support, and we should respond to that need, rather than ignoring it and responding only to the inappropriate behaviour.

It can be hard for some children to tolerate their feelings and this can result in them trying to get rid of them rather than accepting and trying to understand and process them. For example, a child who is unable to manage feeling angry may hit another child or throw something as a way of trying to get rid of that feeling. When a child picks on or bullies another child, it may make them feel big and powerful and can be an opportunity for them to feel strong, albeit for a short amount of time. Children need help and support from adults to realise that it is natural to have feelings and that they can be helped to understand how to

DOI: 10.4324/9781003379751-2

recognise and express them. It can be useful to integrate positive messages about feelings throughout the school day, such as 'All feelings are useful as they can tell us if something is wrong.' This validates their experiences and normalises how children may be feeling. Some children have little resilience to cope with their feelings, and events that can happen during the course of a school day can feel too difficult for them to manage, such as losing a game or not being at the front of the line.

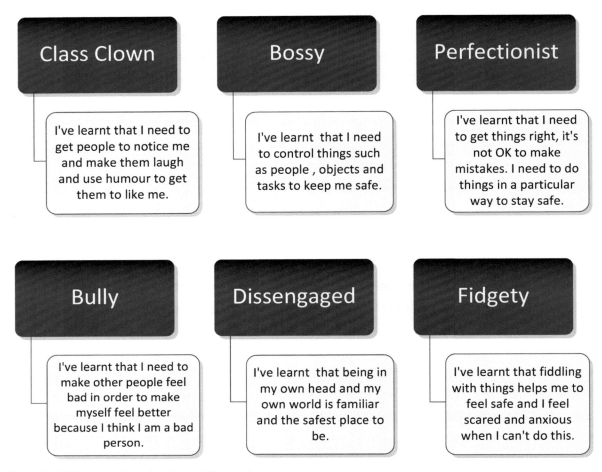

Figure 0.2 What is this behaviour telling us?

The above examples provide possible reasons why children have learnt particular behaviours as coping strategies to deal with their feelings. If a child was able to put those feelings into words, it would be easier for adults to empathise and support them.

Responding to behaviour

It's crucial that school staff try to interpret children's distress behaviour through a caring and compassionate lens and reflect on why they are doing whatever they are doing. What is the child showing you through their behaviour? Are they showing you they feel safe and comfortable or are they showing you they feel unsafe and scared and can't sit still and relax? Inappropriate behaviour is a sign of an unmet need, difficulty coping or a lack of knowledge.

Figure 0.3 Understanding the feelings behind the behaviour

For school staff, it can be a huge challenge to look beyond the behaviour and attempt to understand what the child may be feeling. It can be easy to judge children for their behaviour as the following comments demonstrate:

- He's just attention seeking
- She's being manipulative
- He never stops talking
- She's so immature
- He never speaks
- She never listens

However, if staff are able to meet a child's need to be noticed and remembered in a positive and supportive way, they may reduce or even stop the behaviour. For example, 'I know it's really hard for you to listen carefully so I am going to give you something to remind you and help you to practise this.'

Strategies to help children feel safe in school

- Face – open and warm
- Tone of voice – varied and light rather than stern or monotone, never use sarcasm
- Body language – open and warm rather than folded arms
- Surrender – take responsibility, apologise, be a role model
- Relationship focused – commit to staying in the relationship and working through difficulties

What can you do?

As adults, the more understanding we can have of what a child may be trying to communicate to us through their behaviour, the greater the chance of the child being understood and being able to make sense of their thoughts and feelings. Children are often very alone with overwhelming thoughts and feelings and this can be a lonely and terrifying experience. Children communicate a range of different feelings through their behaviour and these can be expressed in many different ways; for example, if a child is scared, they may hide under the table or pretend they are not bothered. Children bring into the now what they are living through – what are the children bringing into your class? If a child is able to have their feelings accepted, acknowledged and validated without judgment or reprimand by an adult, they learn that all feelings are acceptable and this can impact on their behaviour in a positive way.

You can make a difference

- Use a calm, gentle and nurturing approach with children
- Focus on and ensure children are clear about the behavioural expectations of the school
- Provide frequent opportunities to enable children to feel good about themselves
- Spend extra time with children if and when you can
- Be reflective and curious about children's behaviour and what it may be telling us, rather than just reacting to it
- Provide regular positive messages to children
- Commit to making your school a happier place for everyone

What is reflective language and how does it help?

One of the biggest challenges facing primary school staff can be dealing with children's behaviour in a way that has a positive impact on them, is not detrimental to their self-esteem and enables them to make realistic changes. The use of reflective language which considers and explores the possible reasons behind the behaviour is a useful tool for any member of school staff. Reflective language is a subtle way of providing positive messages to children. It communicates to the child that you are seeing them, trying to understand them and acknowledging any feelings they may be experiencing. It enables adults to tentatively explore the child's experience without making judgements or assumptions about it. For example, 'It can feel frustrating when you put your hand up and I chose another child to answer.' It also provides an opportunity to build a connection and develop a relationship with a child, along with providing a commentary on their behaviour. For example, 'I can see you are trying hard to fit those pieces together.' As with anything you are doing for the first time, it may feel a bit strange at first; however, I encourage you to persevere and experiment with using it.

Reflective language is based on the understanding that all behaviour is a form of communication. When children show us their feelings through their behaviour, it is important that we not only try to understand what they may be feeling and trying to communicate to us, but also that we provide them with an emotional vocabulary to help them talk about their experiences. For example, if a child says they do not want to do something or behaves disruptively, they may be telling us they are scared or anxious. Reflective language provides children with an emotional vocabulary, which in turn can help them to start understanding and expressing how they feel.

Using reflective language clearly communicates to a child 'I see you, I hear you, I am trying to understand you', and thus enables them to feel seen, heard, valued and understood. For some children, this can be a relatively new experience and may result in increased self-worth and self-esteem. By using this with children, adults are providing a positive message to them, 'You are worth thinking about and trying to understand, and I am trying to help you to work out how you feel and support you with understanding and managing your feelings.' It can be beneficial to use reflective language rather than always reprimanding children

DOI: 10.4324/9781003379751-3

or telling them what to do, because it acknowledges and validates the child's feelings and experiences. This is valuable for all children, but especially for children who may not have this experience consistently within their family.

Examples of reflective responses

- 'Sometimes it can feel hard to ask for help'
- 'I can see you look unsure about what to do'
- 'Perhaps you're worried about getting it wrong, but everyone makes mistakes sometimes'
- 'It can feel difficult when I'm not in class'
- 'Maybe you're worried about starting that piece of work'

As you experiment with this form of communication, please remember that the emphasis is on tentatively suggesting what might be going on for the child. We may not know for certain what is behind a child's behaviour, but we are showing them that we are thinking about them, trying to understand them and offering a possible articulation of what they are feeling. Imagine for a minute how differently you might respond to a colleague or friend saying 'You are angry' or 'I am wondering if you are angry.'

When to use it

The use of reflective language can be integrated into the school day. For example, if a child is struggling or finding a task difficult, it can help to reflect 'It can be difficult when we get things wrong' or 'It can feel frustrating when we are trying to do something and we can't work out how to do it.' This enables the child to feel noticed and understood, along with helping them to identify how frustration feels. Over time, this enables the child to link the feelings with the word and to make that connection themselves. This may result in them being able to use the word themselves when they next have that feeling. Providing frequent opportunities for children to hear emotional vocabulary being used in the appropriate context increases the likelihood that they will begin understanding and expressing their feelings more easily. When children are able to express their feelings verbally, it reduces the need for them to show how they feel through their behaviour, thus reducing incidents of behavioural difficulties.

Throughout this book, you are provided with examples of reflective language to experiment with. Each half term, there is a different type of reflective language for you to practice using and there are examples of these at the front of the section for each half term. Each week, I have identified a different one for you to use from the list, but I encourage you to think about the child and use a different one from the list if you feel it's more appropriate for the child. Over time, as you become more confident at using reflective language, you may develop your own examples to use.

Affirmative responses

When a child feels an adult is trying to help and understand them, they may start to feel more positive about themselves, therefore enabling them to make changes to their behaviour. The use of reflective language within schools encourages a sense of safety and security, rather than fear and anxiety. If a child is able to have their feelings accepted, acknowledged and validated without judgment or reprimand by an adult, they learn that all feelings are acceptable and this can impact on their behaviour in a positive way. When a child's behaviour is explored in a gentle and reassuring way by using reflective language, it provides them with an opportunity to begin to acknowledge their own mistakes and gradually learn to start taking responsibility for their actions. These are small but essential steps towards learning about choices and consequences and ultimately making positive changes to their behaviour.

Providing positive messages to a child

I've been thinking about how hard it is for you to remember your PE kit	You are worth thinking about
I'm going to ask Mrs Jones to spend some time with you and teach you how to tie your shoelaces, I can see it frustrates you when you try to do them	You are worth helping
It's important that everyone has a turn at being at the front of the line	Your needs matter
You looked sad when you didn't get chosen for the football team, I wonder if you'd like to choose a friend and help me unpack the new books	You are important

Enabling children to ask for help

When children have learnt self-sufficiency at a young age, they may try to manage on their own, as they have learned 'It's not ok to ask for help, or if you do, no one responds.' A reflection such as 'You may need some help from an adult with this, and I can help you if you would like me to' provides the message that sometimes children need help from an adult and it is acceptable to ask for it. It enables the child to have the choice and decide whether they need help, rather than the adult controlling the situation and deciding for them. This can help to reduce any feelings of anxiety and fear that the child may be having. It is also useful if children see school staff asking for help, as this can be very liberating. For example, 'I'm going to ask Mr Bell to help me with the display because everyone needs help from other people sometimes.'

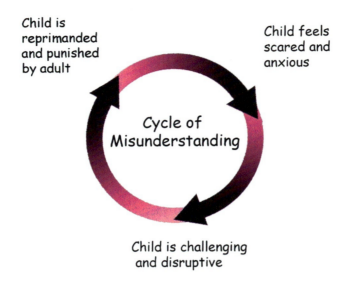

Child is reprimanded and punished by adult

Child feels scared and anxious

Cycle of Misunderstanding

Child is challenging and disruptive

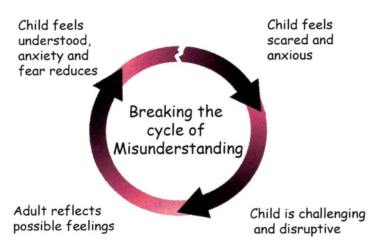

Child feels understood, anxiety and fear reduces

Child feels scared and anxious

Breaking the cycle of Misunderstanding

Adult reflects possible feelings

Child is challenging and disruptive

Figure 0.4 The cycle of misunderstanding

Acknowledging your own feelings

School staff can be positive role models for children when dealing with and expressing their own feelings during the school day as this provides children with concrete experiences of this. This is particularly important for children who may not have this demonstrated to them outside of school, for example, a child who sees their dad punch the wall when they are angry, rather than voicing it. School staff can use opportunities during the school day to admit and acknowledge their own mistakes, for example, 'Even grown-ups get things wrong sometimes.' There are many opportunities during the school day where staff can acknowledge their own feelings where appropriate, for example, 'I felt cross when the photocopier was broken.' Staff can also identify and acknowledge difficult times during the school day, such as, 'It's raining again and that can be frustrating when we were looking forward to doing PE outside.'

Why it's important

The use of reflective language has a positive impact on both children's emotional wellbeing and their behaviour. Some children may find it difficult to express their feelings and may have learnt that it is not safe to do so. Their anxieties may manifest in their behaviour, for example, a child who is unable to sit still or is always fiddling with something. It can help if their feelings and behaviour can be identified and acknowledged in a gentle and supportive way, rather than reprimanding them for not being able to express or manage their feelings, for example, 'I can see that it's really difficult for you to sit still and relax until you know what we are going to do.' This kind of reflection may enable children to manage their anxieties more easily.

Section 1

Settling in

DOI: 10.4324/9781003379751-4

Focus for the half term

For this half term, we are going to be focusing on and thinking about getting to know and build relationships with the children in your class. The first half term is crucial for developing initial relationships and this can often provide the relational template for the rest of the year. The importance of doing this cannot be underestimated. The relationship building process can be time consuming and exhausting, especially at the start of the school year when there are so many other things to do and priorities to attend to. However, the quality of the relationship between the teacher and each child in their class has a profound impact on the child's ability to feel safe and secure at school, which in turn impacts on them feeling settled and engaging fully with their learning.

The relationships between the children in your class also need time and attention during this first half term, especially if there are children who are new to the class, or the classes have been mixed with another class. It is important not to make assumptions about the children's social and emotional skills and their ability to connect with the other children in the class, but to consider where the children are emotionally, as this will impact on their relationships. For example, a nine-year-old who is emotionally much younger may not be able to share and may find working with others very difficult. This relationship focused approach will enable both school staff and children to have a happier and more successful school year.

When you have a new class, you may not know each child's story, what they live with or have experienced and how this has affected them. A child's experiences outside of school will always have a huge impact on them and affect their ability to focus and engage with their learning, along with their ability to develop and maintain relationships. Children's experiences within their families have a fundamental impact on how they see the world and how they feel about themselves and others. Within the family, a child receives constant messages about who they are, their behaviour and what is expected of them, and thus form their initial sense of themselves as people. When these messages are positive, supportive and nurturing, this can result in the child feeling happy, safe, secure, confident and believing in themselves.

However, if the messages from within the family are negative, critical and harsh or indifferent, this can result in the child feeling unhappy, unsafe, insecure and lacking in confidence and self-belief. The child brings these experiences with them into school, which has a profound impact on their relationships, their learning and how they feel about themselves and other people. It is worth spending time thinking about each child's experiences outside of school and observing any interactions between children and their parents and caregivers, as this can provide important information and relevant clues to their behaviour in school. It's imperative that children feel safe and secure at school, and both school and the classroom can become a safe base for children, where they are acknowledged and validated for themselves.

The beginning of the school year can be an anxiety provoking and stressful time for both children and school staff. For school staff, there is often a sense of not having enough time, feeling constantly busy and at times overwhelmed, with a sense of urgency to get tasks completed. The children may return to school after the summer break not having had as many or any boundaries at home, feeling worried about separating from their parents or caregivers, along with the anxiety of being in a new class and wondering what their new teacher will be like. The combination of these thoughts and feelings from staff and children can be taken into the classroom and can create feelings of anxiety and uncertainty for everyone. For each child, their individual life experiences will inform how they experience and cope with this. It's important that all of this is acknowledged to the children, regardless of their age, and reflective language can provide a useful tool to do this and to support this process of you developing new relationships. This first half term is crucial for getting to know and develop relationships with the children and I encourage you to invest as much time as you can in this – you will reap the rewards of this later on in the year.

How children may present

There may be children in your new class who you already know a bit about or you may have heard about from other staff; if this is the case, then try and put any preconceived ideas about them to one side. Beginning with a fresh start enables you both to have the best chance of success at building a new relationship. We can all respond differently to different people, and it can be really useful to acknowledge this to the children so they are not worried about what the previous teacher may have told you. The children in your class will come to you with their own experiences of how adults behave and their own sense of how they see the world. This will have a big impact on their ability to feel settled in their new class and their ability to build a relationship with you. Some of the children will experience the world as feeling safe and secure and adults as being consistent and predictable. These children experience the world as safe, fun and exciting and think that other people are generally nice and kind. They usually feel good about themselves, have a sense of confidence and self-esteem and are able to manage the change to a new class quite easily. These children tend to settle into a new class well, are generally easy to build a relationship with and have friends within the class. They are able to work well independently, in a way that's appropriate to their age, and can also work well with others.

However, other children in your class may have experienced something very different. They may experience the world outside of school as frightening, unsettling and traumatic. They may experience adults as unpredictable, chaotic and overwhelmed. These children can find it hard to feel good about themselves – they may have had periods of their lives where they have been ignored or met with hostility and therefore can find it hard to hold onto and believe positive things about themselves. For these children, the change to a new class and developing a relationship with a new class teacher can be very stressful and frightening. These children may find it harder to manage change and may still be appearing to be unsettled a few weeks into the term. You may find it more difficult to develop a relationship with them and they may also struggle with friendships with the other children. They can appear to be overly independent, perhaps not asking for help at all, or may appear helpless, constantly needing help and unable to do very much on their own. Although these children may be much harder to connect with, they need a consistent, predictable and nurturing relationship with adults more than other children. It can be exhausting having children in your class with this level of emotional and social need, but when you persevere with enabling them to succeed, the rewards are high.

All behaviour from children is a form of communication and provides a useful insight into how they are feeling. It is not always easy to hold this in mind, especially if the child is challenging and confrontational and their behaviour impacts on other children and disrupts the classroom learning. Children don't have the same language skills as adults and are therefore not always able to tell us what is happening or to communicate their needs. They also don't have the same cognitive understanding as adults – they can't always understand why they feel in a particular way and don't understand that most feelings pass. As adults, we know that challenging experiences can pass and that we won't have difficult feelings forever. Children may not have the same understanding of this. Imagine just having the feelings and not knowing why you have them or being able to do anything about them. Children communicate their feelings through their behaviour and it is our task as adults to try and work out what a child is telling us so we can help them with their feelings.

Relationships

In order to help children to feel settled and secure in their new class, spend as much time as you can getting to know them. This can be done in a relaxed and informal way as well as by providing more structured opportunities. If classes have been mixed and the children are not used to being together, it will help to do some work on this too, so they feel like a more cohesive unit. Spending extra time with a child can have a huge impact on them, and investing just five minutes a day can help with this. This could be done at lunchtime, for example, while you are clearing up or setting out the class and can provide children with a different experience of a staff relationship. The child can be involved in helping put out equipment or tidying the classroom and it enables an informal interaction to take place and the relationship to develop. The outcome for the child is beneficial in terms of relationship experience and developing confidence and self-esteem. The sense of purpose and importance developed by offering children the opportunity to help with jobs enables them to feel better about themselves. This is particularly useful for a child who may not have the opportunity to feel good about themselves at other times. For example, a child who finds it hard to sit still and concentrate may not gain the same satisfaction or sense of achievement that another child can who finds this easier to do. However, a note of caution is necessary to ensure that children do not feel they are only of value or importance when they are helping other people, so this needs to be considered when identifying children who may benefit from this additional input.

Situation
• Change, new class, new relationships

Child feels
• Anxious, worried, scared

Adult solution
• Help with feelings by acknowleding, naming, describing, reassuring

Impact
• Anxiety, fear and worry reduce

Child feels
• More settled, relaxed, happy

Result
• Engages with learning, improved relationships, enjoys school

Figure 1.1 The impact of understanding and responding to the child's needs

Possible reasons for their behaviour

We have discussed how change can be very hard for some children, and that developing a new relationship with a new teacher can be difficult. Observe the children in your class and consider how they might be adapting to change. Some children will be worried that you will have unrealistic expectations or may not like them; other children may have heard negative things about you from other children. Remember that for some children who have experienced a lot of unwelcome change in their lives, any kind of change can be extremely stressful and may make them feel unsafe. It is essential that you are clear at the beginning with the whole class that the start of the year is a fresh start for everyone, as this will help to reduce anxiety.

Strategies to try

- Spend time with the whole class talking about the kind of class they want to have, how they want it to feel etc.; depending on their age, encourage them to work in pairs to identify ways they can create this. For example, 'We want to feel relaxed; we can do this by helping each other.'

This can create an experience of class ownership and shared responsibility, along with providing you with a better understanding of the children. This can be done on the first day of term as part of a whole class approach to identifying and creating the class environment you would like to see and they would like to experience.

- If you know you have children who can be very loud, you may want to introduce a noise-ometer, a cardboard barometer on the wall which you can use to encourage the class to use quieter voices.

This provides an opportunity for you to introduce the expectations you have around noise and what you find acceptable. The visual aspect of this enables you to manage this by pointing to it, without constantly repeating yourself or reprimanding an individual child.

- Be consistent and predictable so the children come to know and trust what to expect from you.

When children experience inconsistency and unpredictability on a regular basis, this can increase their anxiety, which may have a negative impact on their classroom engagement as they become preoccupied and anxious about what's happening next. A consistent and predictable approach provides a sense of safety and security, which is particularly important for children who don't experience this outside of school.

- Acknowledge the changes that are occurring as they are happening. For example, 'It can feel really hard and a bit strange at the start of the year as we don't know each other yet, but we will get to know each other the more we spend time together.'

This validates how many of the children may be feeling, enables them to feel less alone and overwhelmed by their own feelings and provides a sense of hope for the future, along with reminding them that difficult feelings don't always last. It's important that children are reminded of this, as they can find it hard to understand that difficult feelings don't last forever.

- Implement a settling in activity with the class where they are encouraged to draw or write about their worries or fears about being in a new class. These can be put in a box for you to look at individually or shared with the class as a discussion. (Keep these as it can be useful to look at them again with the children in the last half term.)

Creating an opportunity for the whole class to do this, along with creating anonymity by putting them in a box, provides a safe space for children to be really open and honest about their feelings. This provides a very different experience to a class discussion and can provide an insight into a child's internal world; for example, a child who writes about being worried about SATs at the start of Year 6.

- Use gentle reminders of whole class behavioural expectations. For example, 'Who can I see that looks ready to listen? Who can I see that looks ready for learning?'

This approach is less 'shaming' than focusing on and naming an individual child who is talking, and is a more nurturing and positive way of managing behaviour. When a child has been judged, criticised and experienced frequent negativity towards them outside of school, highlighting their behaviour in front of the whole class may result in an increase in the behaviour you are trying to get them to stop, as they struggle to manage their feelings about themselves. As adults, we would find it very difficult to manage this public approach to highlighting behaviour we needed to work on – imagine, for example, if this happened during a staff meeting.

- Spend time getting to know them through informal discussions before or after lunch or at the end of the day. For example, 'Let's go around the class and everyone say what their favourite colour/thing to eat is.'

This can be a fun and light-hearted approach which can be a more useful way of getting to know more about the children and helping them to learn about each other. For some children, this approach can enable them to share about themselves in a relaxed way, without the pressure of coming over to talk to you. It also enables you to use this information to connect with children who are quieter and more reserved. Children should be given the opportunity to pass and not contribute if they choose not to, so they feel they have a choice. Being aware of the children who choose this can provide us with useful information about a child.

- Try to think about the meaning behind any behaviour. For example, ask yourself why they are doing something, rather than just looking at what they are doing.

This curious approach to a child's behaviour, rather than just focusing on trying to get a child to stop, can result in longer-lasting changes for the child. Reflecting on how the child may be feeling and wondering why they may be doing something can provide a useful insight into the child. For example, If a child is frequently looking out of the window, think about why they may be doing it. Are they finding their work too difficult? Are they worried about what may be happening at home? By being more curious about a child's behaviour, we may be able to respond to it with more empathy and understanding, which in turn will help the child to change it.

- Address things specifically as they occur rather than leaving things, as they may develop into something bigger. For example, 'I've noticed you seem to be finding it hard to remember what we're doing – I wonder if I can do anything to help you with this?'

This enables the children to feel they have a voice and are seen, heard and understood. It also provides a positive message about being helped and conveys to them you are willing to do this.

- Be aware that the return to school and the transition between home and school can be a difficult experience for some children. Highlight the differences between school and home wherever possible. For example, 'At home, you may be able to choose when you eat your lunch or have more say in what you're eating, but in school...'

This can assist children with understanding the key differences and help to reduce their anxiety as they are able to understand why they may be feeling worried or unsettled.

- Create a script for staff who are providing cover in your absence. Include general information about how to respond to behaviour and class expectations, along with specific details about any children you know will find the change difficult.

This provides a uniformed approach and creates consistency and predictability. This can help children feel more settled and secure in class and helps the other member of staff to be more informed.

- Ensure each child ends the day on a positive note, especially if there have been any difficulties during the day. For example, tell the class you are looking forward to seeing them the next day or after the weekend.

This increases the likelihood of a child having a more positive day when they come back to school, rather than worrying about whether the school staff will still be cross with them. It's important that children leave school with good feelings about themselves wherever possible.

- Create a quiet, calm area within the classroom so children are able to have some space and time if and when they need it. Avoid using this for time out or consequences, as it gives mixed messages to children.

This provides an opportunity for children to practice self-regulation and enables them to have a safe space within class to do this.

- Create a visual 'Who is looking after us today' timetable with photos of members of staff attached with Velcro so they can be moved if needed. Display this in a place where all children can see it and go through it before and after lunch when you are going through the daily timetable.

This can provide an increased feeling of security and stability for all the children, but is particularly important for children who are relationship focused or who have experienced relational loss.

- Design a feelings chart using faces or words for children to describe how they feel when they arrive at school and after lunch. Provide each child with a tag with their name, which they can attach to the particular feeling they are experiencing. Start with 'happy', 'sad', 'cross' and 'scared' and increase the list with 'worried', 'frustrated' 'disappointed' as their understanding of their emotions increases.

This creates an opportunity to regularly check how each child is feeling and can be easier than asking them. This provides them with a regular experience of describing how they feel and can increase their emotional literacy.

- If a child finds it difficult to sit still on the carpet, make them a carpet spot out of cardboard, allowing them to decorate it and show them how to sit with their legs and arms inside the circle. Ensure there is plenty of space for the child to achieve success with this.

This enables a child to practise and they can be encouraged by regular praise and acknowledgement. Encourage the child to take responsibility for getting the mat and putting it away, along with identifying when they feel ready to practise without using it.

- Understand that their behaviour is trying to tell you something and communicate to them that you are trying to understand this. For example, 'I can see you are really angry and I'm wondering why that is?'

This gentle and inquisitive approach provides a positive message to the child about being seen and that you are trying to understand them. If you are able to respond with curiosity and acknowledgement of their feelings, a child may find it easier to communicate with you about what's happening and the feelings they are experiencing.

Questions to think about/reflections towards the end of the half term

- How am I feeling about this class?
- How well has the class settled?
- How happy am I with the classroom environment?
- Do I want to make any changes, for example, moving furniture?
- Which children do I feel connected to and why?
- Which children do I feel I don't know very well and why?
- What can I do to get to know those children more?

End-of-half-term summaries

- Spending quality time building relationships and getting to know children impacts greatly on their experience of school life
- Children's experiences within their family are key to understanding their behaviour and their ability to develop and sustain relationships
- Stress and anxiety for both children and staff need to be acknowledged. Using reflective language is a useful tool to do this
- Children communicate their thoughts and feelings through their behaviour
- Staff being curious and considering the possible reasons and feelings behind a child's behaviour can help them gain a better understanding of the needs of the child

Week 1

Reflection:
It can be a bit difficult being in a new class because
we don't know each other yet.

Child:
Presenting behaviour:

Planned strategies:

What worked?

What could be better?

How has this impacted on how I feel?

Remember:
Focus on building relationships and getting to know your class.

Week 2

Reflection:
It can feel very hard not to interrupt, but remember
we are practising listening to each other.

Child:
Presenting behaviour:

Planned strategies:

What worked?

What could be better?

How has this impacted on how I feel?

Remember:
Some children find transition hard; stress and
anxiety show in many different ways.

Week 3

Reflection:
It can feel hard when you don't know me and
don't know what to expect.

Child:
Presenting behaviour:

Planned strategies:

What worked?

What could be better?

How has this impacted on how I feel?

Remember:
We need to spend time getting to know and understand children if we are going to help them.

Week 4

Reflection:
It can feel frustrating when we try and
do something and it doesn't work.

Child:
Presenting behaviour:

Planned strategies:

What worked?

What could be better?

How has this impacted on how I feel?

 Remember:
Some children take longer to build relationships and
settle into a new class.

Week 5

Reflection:
It can feel disappointing when we do something
wrong, but everyone makes mistakes sometimes.

Child:
Presenting behaviour:

Planned strategies:

What worked?

What could be better?

How has this impacted on how I feel?

Remember:
Focus on getting to know and understand the child, rather than just trying to change their behaviour.

Week 6

Reflection:
It can feel hard when other children
are praised for their work.

Child:
Presenting behaviour:

Planned strategies:

What worked?

What could be better?

How has this impacted on how I feel?

Remember:
Change can be difficult for lots of children.

Week 7

Reflection:
It can feel very frustrating when you are
finding it hard to understand something.

Child:
Presenting behaviour:

Planned strategies:

What worked?

What could be better?

How has this impacted on how I feel?

Remember:
Authenticity is crucial to building trust and making a connection with children.

Week 8

Reflection:
It can feel unfair when someone else gets
chosen to do something you want to do.

Child:
Presenting behaviour:

Planned strategies:

What worked?

What could be better?

How has this impacted on how I feel?

Remember:
Trust is the foundation of relationships; it can be very hard for children who haven't any experience of this.

Use this space to review the half term – you may want to think about what worked well, what you would do again in the future and any new ideas or things to try.

Section 2

Christmas festivities

DOI: 10.4324/9781003379751-5

Focus for the half term

For this half term, we are going to be focusing on and thinking about the impact of the Christmas festivities and how this can affect the children in your class. As this time of year usually brings lots of changes to the daily routine, along with the addition of extra activities that need to be included, it can be a stressful and exhausting time for both adults and children in school. Some children may find this half term particularly difficult and it's crucial to remember that Christmas may not be a positive experience for all children. Many children love Christmas and get very excited about it, often several weeks beforehand. For these children, Christmas can be a positive and enjoyable experience, involving spending time at home with family and possibly extended family, and can be a generally happy time. However, some of the children in your class may have a completely different experience, and it's important for school staff to be mindful of these children throughout this half term. There is usually an increase in alcohol consumption, conflicts and domestic violence at this time of year, as families are under huge pressures and stress, and there may be children in your class who are affected by this.

There may also be children who don't celebrate Christmas at all and staff need to be aware of and sensitive to these cultural and religious differences. For children who don't celebrate Christmas, being part of some of the events in school may be uncomfortable, and school staff should always make sure they are aware of these children and are supportive in meeting their needs too. It can also be useful for school staff to reflect on their own thoughts and feelings about the festive period. For some school staff, Christmas can be a time of immense sadness as they grieve for people that are no longer with them due to relationship breakdowns or bereavements. All these factors are useful to be aware of during this time.

Profile checklist

- Finding it hard to manage the changes in class, such as wall displays and decorations being put up
- Constantly asking questions and needing to know what will be happening next
- More fragile and less resilient than usual, for example, crying easily
- Falling out with friends and struggling with peer relationships
- Non-compliance or refusal to participate in the celebrations, such as the Christmas performance
- Sabotaging the celebrations by being disruptive or challenging in order to try and miss being involved in them
- Getting over-excited easily and lacking ability to self-regulate
- Generally being more unsettled, tired, worried or anxious
- Changes in behaviour ranging from quiet and withdrawn to angry and aggressive

How children may present

As the Christmas break approaches and the festivities in school increase, there may be children in your class who start to show you they find this time of year very difficult. It is crucial to be aware of this and ensure that you and other school staff find time to acknowledge this, otherwise it can reinforce the sense of isolation and loneliness and feelings of being different in a negative way for the children. Some children may be able to articulate their feelings about this time of year and may say things like 'I hate Christmas' or 'I wish Christmas was over'. However, other children, especially younger ones, may not be able to express their feelings and you will just see the changes in their behaviour. These changes can be helped by school staff being curious about the possible reasons for the behaviour, and acknowledging the feelings that the children may be experiencing. For children who are looked after or adopted, Christmas can be a challenging time as they may be reminded of previous years when they have lived with birth families and siblings. They may need additional support, reassurance and nurture as they try to manage feelings of loss, sadness, anger and upset which they may be experiencing. This can also be helped by school staff acknowledging this, if it's appropriate for the child, and checking with the adoptive parent or foster carer before doing this.

Relationships

You may notice some changes in the children's behaviour; some may be quite subtle, such as being more detached and distant, whereas others will be more visible, such as becoming clingier. For some children, the thought of being away from school for two weeks can be very difficult and they may respond to the onset of this by being upset or angry with you, or generally being more disruptive. The friendships and relationships between the children in your class may become more unsettled and you may experience some children having more conflicts and reacting more easily. Be aware of your own levels of tiredness and stress at this time of year as this will also impact on the children.

If your school does a Christmas performance, be aware that some children's parents or carers may not come to watch them and consider how this may feel for them and look out for any comments from other children about this. The experience of being involved in a Christmas performance may be challenging for some children, depending on their levels of confidence and self-esteem – being in the spotlight and being 'seen' by lots of people can be anxiety provoking and may create feelings of shame for some children who find it hard to manage this. If school staff are able to respond to this with empathy and reassurance, it can help to reduce a child's feelings of not being good enough and can help to increase their resilience and the likelihood of them managing this experience well. It can be hard to do this when staff are under pressure themselves to put on a performance which includes all the children.

Possible reasons for their behaviour

For some children, there may be negative associations with Christmas and therefore this time of year can be very difficult for them. In some families, Christmas can be a time of huge additional stress, with financial and relational pressures on families. Some children may experience Christmas as a time of sadness, stress and upset with the increased adult use of alcohol, pressure for families to spend time together and potential for an increase in domestic violence. Therefore, not surprisingly, as soon as the Christmas festivities are mentioned in school, there can be resistance and ambivalence from some children. The excitement of Christmas, the sense of uncertainty and the promise of lots of presents, and a generally happy time may create additional challenges for children who find it hard to regulate their behaviour and manage their feelings. This can also be true for children who don't have positive experiences of the festive period, as the unpredictable aspect may create fear and anxiety for them.

Self-regulation is an important skill that helps children to manage their feelings and behaviour. For a child to be able to regulate their own stress levels, they need to have had this experience from an adult. For example, when a baby cries, the adults respond with love and concern and help to soothe and reduce stress levels. Over time as this pattern repeats, the baby gradually starts to develop their own stress regulation system and can start to tolerate difficult feelings more easily. As the baby develops, they are able to self-soothe in an appropriate way and develop self-regulation. However, if the baby is ignored or met with hostility when they cry, their stress levels increase. The adult response to the baby either prevents or helps them to develop their own stress regulation system.

Children in school who can find it hard to manage their feelings, whether it's fear, anxiety or excitement, will benefit from some extra support with this from a consistent, caring adult. The feeling of excitement can be a difficult one for some children to manage – they can experience it in their body in a similar way to feeling anxious. If a child is showing they are finding it hard to manage excitement, they may need additional help from a patient adult to help them practise having the feeling and learning to self-regulate. If an adult gets cross or frustrated with a child who is getting over-excited, this can increase their anxiety and make them less able to self-regulate.

Staff self-care

Working in schools is a challenging but rewarding job which can be physically and emotionally draining. School staff are often juggling multiple tasks and demands and can be working in stressful situations. This is particularly relevant during this half term, which is extremely busy and stressful, with a huge amount of pressure on school staff to be able to manage even more than they usually do. There are often expectations that staff are able to create and put on a performance, ranging from singing carols to a full nativity show. Teachers are expected to be good at so many different things all the time, and this half term can really highlight this. It's crucial that school staff try and practice some self-care around this time to build their resilience and support their own wellbeing. This can include staff trying to make extra time for themselves and making looking after themselves a priority, although at times this can feel like an impossible task. School staff are usually really good at taking care of other people, but if they don't look after themselves, it can be so much harder to look after others.

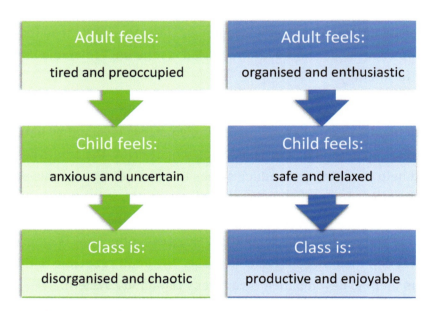

Figure 2.1 How adults' feelings can impact on the child

Strategies to try

- Acknowledge that Christmas can be a difficult and stressful time of the year and observe any children who respond, either verbally or non-verbally, to this statement.

By doing this, you are putting into words how many of the children and staff may be feeling, which creates an experience of normalising feelings. Children can often feel very alone and isolated with their feelings, which can increase their feelings of anxiety and overwhelm. Suggesting they are not alone with their feelings and acknowledging that other people may feel the same, including adults, can create a sense of relief for them.

- Acknowledge that not everyone has a good time or enjoys Christmas and reassure them it's ok if they feel like this.

There can be such pressure on everyone to see and experience Christmas in a positive way, which comes from television, social media etc. Some children may fear or feel anxious about the festive season, perhaps linked to past negative experiences of witnessing domestic violence or a family bereavement, and it's crucial for these children that their experience is acknowledged and validated.

- Validate any feelings that are expressed. For example, 'It sounds like you don't like Christmas and that's ok, not everyone enjoys or likes it.'

It can take courage for a child to express their feelings of dislike or ambivalence, especially if they are going against the feelings of most of the other children. By validating a child's feelings, you are providing them with reassurance and acceptance, which helps them feel more secure about themselves.

- Try not to dismiss or discount a child's feelings. Don't say 'Oh, everyone loves Christmas.'

When a child's feelings are dismissed or discounted, they may feel bad about themselves or experience feelings of shame. This reaction could prevent them from expressing their feelings in the future as they may think they have done something wrong. This may result in them feeling it's not ok to say how they really feel and can lead to them changing what they say in order to fit in and be accepted.

- Offer children a countdown calendar for the return to school, a variation on an advent calendar, that they can take home with them and have over the Christmas period.

This can be useful for all children, but particularly those who experience school as a safe place and find it hard being at home. For some children, the visual aspect of being able to see the return to school and when it will happen can provide a sense of certainty during what may be an uncertain time, with lots of changes.

- For younger children up to Year 2, who are still finding it hard to settle or return to school after the weekend, offer them a booklet with a few pages of them enjoying specific aspects of the school day, for example, playing outside, having lunch with friends or enjoying an activity. Encourage them to take this home and look at it with their parent/carer before returning to school after the festive period.

This creates positive reminders of things they enjoy and can create good feelings they associate with school. This can have a positive impact on their return and help them settle and adjust more easily. I suggest this at this time of the school year as the Christmas break is usually longer than other breaks and can involve seeing lots of people and being very busy.

- Keep naming and describing what's happening. For example, 'It's all feeling a bit difficult at the moment, one minute we are in class doing literacy and the next minute we are in the hall practising our show.'

There are often so many changes happening in school during this half term, especially over the last two weeks, and this can create anxiety and stress for even the most settled children. Talking about these changes can enable children to manage them more easily.

- Make the Christmas schedule as clear and predictable as you can. Keep repeating and explaining what's happening, tell them, draw it, repeat it.

Some children need constant repetition of changes, especially if Christmas is anxiety provoking for them. The pattern of this repetitive cycle provides predictability and clarity to help reduce the children's stress levels.

- Ensure you use a visual timetable to show any changes and keep revisiting this with the class throughout the school day.

Many children find visual timetables useful, and providing such a timetable during this period of immense change can help children to follow what is happening more easily. Children are unable to remember things as easily as adults and the constant changes occurring can create additional anxiety and worry that can easily be addressed by frequent explanations and visual reminders.

- If a child is lacking in confidence and has low self-esteem, create a book of positive things where school staff identify and write something positive about the child in their book in the morning, after break and during the afternoon. The child can decorate the book and take a photocopy of it home on a Friday.

This activity enables school staff to collect a book of positive observations which can be shared with the child on a regular basis, especially when a child is struggling with their behaviour or finding something difficult. This easily accessible tool quickly boosts a child's confidence and self-belief.

- If a child finds it hard to self-regulate and is calling out frequently or finding it hard to wait, create a regular opportunity for them to do some stop/start colouring with an adult. For example, the child is encouraged to colour and respond quickly to the stop-and-start instructions given by the adult.

This opportunity to practise responding to instructions can enable a child to practise and develop self-regulation in a relaxed and informal way. The child can then practise transferring this skill back to class, for example, waiting before responding.

- If a child is regularly fiddling with an object or their shoe, clothing or carpet, give them something to fiddle with, such as a finger puppet, a small amount of Blu Tac or a small stone or object.

When a child is frequently touching things, it can help them if an adult facilitates them being able to do this, rather than moving the child or the object. Allowing a child to have an object (with rules and boundaries about how it's used) can greatly reduce anxiety and therefore increase their concentration and ability to engage with their learning.

- Create a worry box containing small pieces of paper, which is easily accessible for children to use. Encourage children to write or draw on these and put them in the worry box, with the option to be anonymous. Check the box a few times a week and use the contents for class discussions, encouraging the class to identify solutions if they are able to.

This enables children to share their worries in a less intimidating and exposing environment, therefore increasing the likelihood of a child sharing. The class discussions provide an ideal opportunity for the school staff to assess children who need additional support with understanding and to allow them to express their feelings.

- Make time to do a pause-for-a-minute activity at regular times during the day, use a visual sand timer or one on the whiteboard.

Children can easily become overwhelmed and very excited at this time of year, and this is exacerbated for children who find it hard to manage their feelings and to self-regulate. Providing frequent opportunities to help them feel calm and soothed can help them become more aware of these feelings and also provides the children with an opportunity to practise self-regulation.

- Provide calming, soothing music as a background when children are working or engaging in Christmas activities.

This can provide a helpful antidote to any Christmas music and can help children to relax and feel peaceful. Creating frequent opportunities for this can be particularly helpful for children who find it hard to self-regulate.

- Acknowledge, name and describe any possible feelings the children may be having. For example, 'It can feel frightening and worrying when we do our Christmas show in front of the whole school' or 'It can be really hard feeling left out if you don't celebrate Christmas.'

It can be very exposing to participate in a school performance and this may feel overwhelming and anxiety provoking for some children. They may be worried about getting it wrong, being watched by other people or whether their parent or carer will attend. When an adult can put these feelings into words for a child, it can help the child manage these feelings more easily.

Questions to think about/reflections towards the end of the half term

- How am I feeling about this half term?
- How do I feel about the festive period?
- How are my stress levels?
- What can I do to create a more relaxing atmosphere in the classroom?
- How can I get support from others?
- How can I support myself?

End-of-half-term summaries

- Be aware of the increased stress and anxiety for staff and children at this time of year
- Remember that Christmas evokes different feelings for everyone, and isn't necessarily a positive time
- Identify and respond to children who show any behavioural changes
- Look out for and support children who need help with self-regulation
- Practice and increase staff self-care to develop resilience and maintain wellbeing

Week 1

Reflection:
I'm wondering if it would be useful if I explained that again.

Child:
Presenting behaviour:

Planned strategies:

What worked?

What could be better?

How has this impacted on how I feel?

Remember:
Focus on the behaviour you want to see more of.

Week 2

Reflection:
I'm wondering if you would like some help with that;
everyone needs help sometimes.

Child:
Presenting behaviour:

Planned strategies:

What worked?

What could be better?

How has this impacted on how I feel?

Remember:
Be someone who can be wrong and apologise to children.

Week 3

Reflection:
I'm wondering if it can be frustrating when other children finish their work before you.

Child:
Presenting behaviour:

Planned strategies:

What worked?

What could be better?

How has this impacted on how I feel?

Remember:
A child's behaviour is always trying to tell us something.

Week 4

Reflection:
I'm wondering if it's really hard today because it's been raining and we had to stay inside.

Child:
Presenting behaviour:

Planned strategies:

What worked?

What could be better?

How has this impacted on how I feel?

Remember:
Children need help and support from a caring adult to manage feelings of failure and disappointment.

Week 5

Reflection:
I'm wondering if it's hard to remember when
I give you lots of instructions.

Child:
Presenting behaviour:

Planned strategies:

What worked?

What could be better?

How has this impacted on how I feel?

Remember:
It's crucial that we help children to understand and express their feelings.

Week 6

Reflection:
I'm wondering if it would help if I sat nearer to you at carpet time.

Child:
Presenting behaviour:

Planned strategies:

What worked?

What could be better?

How has this impacted on how I feel?

Remember:
Anxiety can be shown in many different and unusual ways.

Week 7

Reflection:
I'm wondering if it's hard when we have to keep
practising our Christmas performance.

Child:
Presenting behaviour:

Planned strategies:

What worked?

What could be better?

How has this impacted on how I feel?

Remember:
Christmas busyness and change of routine can create anxiety for children.

Week 8

Reflection:
I'm wondering if it's unsettling when we do lots of different things for Christmas and our day is different.

Child:
Presenting behaviour:

Planned strategies:

What worked?

What could be better?

How has this impacted on how I feel?

Remember:
Christmas isn't great for all children.

Use this space to review the half term – you may want to think about what worked well, what you would do again in the future and any new ideas or things to try.

Section 3
Cementing relationships

DOI: 10.4324/9781003379751-6

Focus for the half term

For this half term, we are going to be thinking about cementing and affirming the relationships you are developing with your class. At this stage in the school year, you have had the class for a term and may feel like you know some of the children really well but be unsure about others. For some children, developing a connection with their class teacher or any other adults in school can feel like a frightening and overwhelming experience, and they feel wary and unsure. Other children may find this much easier to do and may be more relaxed and therefore easier to connect with. It's important to be aware of children who find it harder to build relationships and to invest time doing this. We will be thinking about how you can do this, along with continuing to help the children to feel safe, settled and secure in your class.

Profile checklist

- Children who experience unpredictable and inconsistent responses from their parents and carers have a distorted relational template
- The child's parents or carers may feel overwhelmed by their own needs and find it hard to think about or try to meet the child's emotional needs
- This may result in the child thinking they need to please the adults in school in order for the adults to like them and want to spend time with them
- This can also result in the child being guarded and unsure, resulting in them being more distant from the adult and unsure about how or if they want to connect with them

How children may present

By the time children start school, they have already received strong messages about themselves, other people and the world. They form their initial sense of themselves and how they are perceived as people from within the family, and this can be either positive or negative. A child's internal rule book is developed early, along with their template of how to build and manage relationships, and how adults respond and behave. The family model's ways of managing feelings providing children with experiences which they bring to school and use in their daily life. All of this occurs within the family, which can be seen as the child's first classroom. Children need familiarity, consistency and predictability in order to help them feel safe and secure. How many children experience this outside of school?

When a child feels safe and secure, they are able to explore freely and have a natural curiosity and excitement about life. We can see the results of this experience in those children who settle quickly, adjust to school life, manage changes comfortably and are generally enthusiastic and engaged with their learning. These children have learnt that they are worth thinking about and caring for, which results in them having high self-esteem and generally feeling positive about themselves. They may present in school as having the skills and ability to build and maintain relationships and respond positively to help and support when it is offered. These children experience adults as being consistent and predictable, which impacts on their ability to develop relationships with school staff. They often find initiating and developing relationships with other children to be straightforward and can have a relaxed and confident approach to this.

However, if a child has had an erratic, inconsistent and unpredictable experience of adult relationships, they may find it more difficult to internalise a sense of feeling safe and secure, and may experience relationships with adults as frightening and unreliable. These children may feel they are not worthwhile as their needs have not been met on a consistent basis. This may result in them feeling negatively about themselves and have a detrimental effect on their ability to develop relationships with adults in school. They can often find initiating and developing relationships with other children to be difficult too and can either be challenging and confrontational or unsure and unconfident at this. When children do not feel safe and secure, it impacts on their social and emotional development as well as their ability to settle and engage with their learning at school. They may be preoccupied with fear and anxiety which can affect their ability to try things and practice and develop new skills. If a child has had a difficult and unhappy time over the Christmas holiday, they may return to school behaving differently from how they were over the previous term. This may include a child being quieter and more withdrawn or more aggressive and confrontational. These behavioural changes may be an indicator that Christmas has been a challenging time, and providing gentle support towards resettling into school life can help a child feel happier and less anxious.

Relationships

One of the joys of working in schools can be the opportunity to build relationships with children in an informal manner. These snapshot conversations that take place during the day and give us an insight into children's lives are so important for our relationship building. It can be very difficult to retain any of this information, let alone remember to ask about it again. However, if we are able to do this, it can have a huge impact. As adults, we know how it feels if someone remembers to ask us about something we have shared with them – we feel listened to, understood and validated for being important and worth thinking about and remembering. Imagine how powerful this would feel to a child, especially a child who is not used to this happening; think about how good it may make them feel. For a child who is not used to adults outside of school showing them much interest, it can make them feel special and interesting if an adult in school asks them if the dog is better now or how their new baby brother is doing. The powerful messages behind this approach to a child are 'you matter', 'you are worth thinking about', 'I care about you' and many others, which can all be new experiences for some children.

These positive and nurturing approaches can transform a child's relational experience and provide them with a strong base from which to build further healthy relationships. School is an ideal place to implement this relationship focused approach and enable children to both experience and practise developing new ways of relating to adults and children. The time, thought and energy invested in this for children will have a lifelong impact on them.

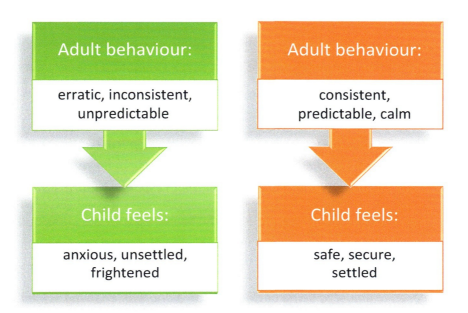

Figure 3.1 The impact of adult behaviour

Possible reasons for their behaviour

The festive season brings expectations and internal and external pressures, along with previous experiences of Christmas which may have been positive or negative. Some of the children in your class may have had a difficult and challenging time over the break and may be relieved to come back to school. However, they may also bring their feelings of hurt, upset and anger back to school with them. For some children, the parent's response to them may be harsh, punitive or inconsistent and if the parent doesn't attempt to repair the relationship, the child experiences overwhelming and unmanageable shame. When children experience this, it becomes tied up with the child's sense of identity and they may feel 'I am a bad person' rather than 'I have done something bad'. Instead of developing guilt, a healthy emotion that helps us to make amends, the child gets stuck in shame. When a child feels shame, they may lie ('I didn't do it'), blame ('It's his fault') or rage ('You always blame me, I'm rubbish'). These feelings can be hard for the child to tolerate and may feel overwhelming for some children. This can result in a negative spiral of self-deprecation and self-loathing. Christmas can put a great deal of pressure and emotional and financial strain on families, and it's important to remember that the festive period may not have been a fun and enjoyable experience for some of the children in your class. It's crucial to hold this in mind when asking children about their Christmas. A more generic 'Welcome back to school, it's nice to see you, what have you been up to' can be a more appropriate general approach, rather than 'Did you have a nice Christmas?'

Strategies to try

- Accept, acknowledge and validate children's feelings rather than dismissing or discounting them. For example, when a child says, 'I've got no friends, everyone hates me', instead of responding with 'That's not true, James likes you', try saying 'That must be so hard to feel like that.'

This response helps the child to feel seen and heard and develop trust in their relationship with school staff. When a child shares how they feel and is vulnerable in this way, it's crucial they feel the adults have really understood their pain and that their response confirms this.

- To help children reconnect with school after the break, do a whole class quiz with children, asking them questions related to being in school, our class and expectations. For example, 'What do you do if I ask a question?' or 'What do you do if the fire alarm goes off?'

This can help children to adjust to being back in school, along with enabling school staff to identify any gaps in a child's understanding of class expectations and school rules. Implementing this activity in a relaxed and lighthearted way will be less anxiety provoking for the class.

- Avoid shouting or raising your voice unless it's essential, instead, when you would like them to stop and listen, just hold your hand up and don't speak, and wait for all the class to stop talking.

If a child has experienced adults shouting and raising their voices frequently, or witnessed domestic violence, any adult who shouts or raises their voice will evoke a response of fear and anxiety in the child. A more regulated response will decrease anxiety levels and create a calmer and more relaxed atmosphere

- If it feels like it's getting loud in class, respond with 'I'm wondering if we can turn the volume down a bit' or 'It's quite noisy and I'm just trying to work out where the noise is coming from.'

This general response is more useful and less shaming than highlighting and naming individual children, and provides the same message that you would like the children to change their behaviour.

- Leave a note for a supply teacher with guidelines for children that need extra help. For example, 'Dante finds it hard if he doesn't know how to start something, ensure you check in with him straight after giving out the task.'

This ensures consistency, provides a framework for a new person to follow and can help the children to feel more safe and secure. It may also mean that it's easier for the class teacher when they return to the class.

- If a child finds it hard to start working, encourage them to write one sentence or do one equation and then tell you. Increase this to two or three etc. as the child's confidence increases.

For some children, the fear of getting something wrong or making a mistake can be debilitating and may result in them being frozen with fear. By setting very small and achievable targets, a child can experience feelings of success and can be motivated by an adult to continue. Over time, this can result in self-motivation as their self-belief increases.

- If a child persistently tells lies, denies they have done something you have seen them do or frequently blames other children, acknowledge 'It can be so hard to say what's happened, maybe you're really scared I will be cross if you tell me the truth, but I'd like you to think about what happened and we will talk about it again later.'

Some children, especially those who have experienced trauma, can have a distorted sense of reality and are overwhelmed with feelings of fear and shame. The feelings of shame or expectation of a negative adult response can be so unbearable that they are unable to logically think through what has just happened. Providing time and a gentle and inquisitive approach can reduce those feelings for the child.

- Create a 'kind hands' chart (similar to a behaviour chart) for a child who finds it hard to keep their hands to themselves or is often hurting other children. This can be divided into several slots for each lesson and is clearly explained to the child beforehand to check their understanding.

This enables a child to experience success frequently and immediately during the day and acts as a motivator for them to increase this behaviour. It also enables school staff to ensure the child has understood the behavioural expectation, along with identifying any times of the day that may be more difficult for the child to manage, such as lunchtime.

- If a child finds it hard to remember more than one instruction, is often behind or is disengaged, it can help to write instructions on a whiteboard for them to work through on their own, rather than frequently asking school staff or disrupting others.

This can create an experience of independence and can be motivating as a child wipes the tasks off the board as they complete them. This also reduces the likelihood of them getting things wrong as they try to remember.

- If a child ignores you or puts their head down when you speak to them, acknowledge this. For example, 'I know it's hard, I can see you putting your head down, maybe it's difficult for you to hear what I'm saying, but I need you to...'

This can reduce a child's feelings of shame, anxiety and overwhelm and enable them to maintain a connection with the adult. It also ensures the child has the expected behaviour reinforced for them.

- Think about the children's emotional as well as chronological age to help you understand and respond to their emotional needs.

When children have experienced difficulties in their life, it can often result in them missing out on some of the key developmental stages they need to experience. This can impact on their emotional needs in particular as they may feel more vulnerable, have less resilience and lack confidence and self-esteem. This can impact them in lots of ways, particularly their ability to connect with school staff.

- Positive, consistent and nurturing relationships reduce fear and anxiety and enable children to feel safe.

When relationships are predictable and caring and provide certainty, children are more able to settle and engage with their learning and enjoy school life. They are more likely to relax and feel less stressed and overwhelmed, resulting in them developing trust in the adults in school.

- Create an environment where children feel safe enough to and are encouraged to make mistakes by ensuring you model this yourself. For example, 'I've written the wrong date on the board today, but that's ok, everyone makes mistakes, even grown-ups.'

This message provides an ideal opportunity for children to fully understand the concept of telling the truth and the importance of admitting our faults. The feelings associated with getting things wrong, such as shame, fear and being not good enough, can be almost unbearable for some children to tolerate. Creating a safe space where adults admit making mistakes is more likely to encourage children to do this, and to practice tolerating painful and difficult feelings.

- Encourage children who stare into space and disconnect easily with gentle reminders. For example, 'I'm wondering if I should explain that again, it can be hard to remember things sometimes.'

This empathic response enables a child to slowly reconnect with the present moment and is more likely to create feelings of safety rather than fear and disengagement.

- Focus on the behaviour you would like to see more of and acknowledge and praise it. For example, 'That's much better, well done for making the change I asked for.'

This positive and nurturing response can create positive feelings for a child, enabling them to feel good about themselves and resulting in them being more likely to want to repeat the behaviour, rather than a response where a child feels bad about themselves, feels more anxious and is unable to manage the feelings this can create, resulting in a more negative response.

- Choose a child you feel would benefit from some extra adult input and choose one thing you could do each day for a week to provide a positive message to them. For example, acknowledge something positive about them, remember something about them and share it with them or ask something about them.

This extra relational top-up will be invaluable for some children who have not had this experience outside of school and can result in increased feelings of self-worth and self-belief for the child, along with other positive feelings about themselves.

Questions to think about/reflections towards the end of the half term

- How well have the class settled back to school after the break?
- Are there any children I'm concerned about?
- Which children do I need to prioritize spending time with?
- How am I feeling after my own Christmas?
- Do I need to get support or ask for help from anyone with this?

End-of-half-term summaries

- Be aware of the impact of a negative experience of Christmas on a child's behaviour and wellbeing
- Children initially develop a relational template based on their experiences with adults outside of school
- This initial experience impacts on their future relationships with adults and children
- School staff can change children's experiences of adult relationships through their approach and responses
- Prioritise cementing and building relationships with the children in your class

Week 1

Reflection:
Perhaps it's difficult to follow the class rules,
I wonder what I can do to help you.

Child:
Presenting behaviour:

Planned strategies:

What worked?

What could be better?

How has this impacted on how I feel?

Remember:
Christmas may not have been enjoyable for all children. Focus on reconnecting with them.

Week 2

Reflection:
Perhaps it feels a bit easier being in my class
now that we know each other better.

Child:
Presenting behaviour:

Planned strategies:

What worked?

What could be better?

How has this impacted on how I feel?

Remember:
It's important to try and understand a child's behaviour in the context of their experience.

Week 3

Reflection:
Perhaps it's hard for you when I ask you not to shout out,
let's see if you can try and practise waiting your turn.

Child:
Presenting behaviour:

Planned strategies:

What worked?

What could be better?

How has this impacted on how I feel?

Remember:
Consider the child's emotional age, not just the chronological age, and how this may affect their behaviour.

Week 4

Reflection:
Perhaps it would help if I gave you more time to finish that,
it can feel hard when we have to rush.

Child:
Presenting behaviour:

Planned strategies:

What worked?

What could be better?

How has this impacted on how I feel?

Remember:
Making time for children may help them feel better about themselves.

Week 5

Reflection:
Perhaps you are finding it hard to concentrate today,
maybe it would help if you got a drink of water.

Child:
Presenting behaviour:

Planned strategies:

What worked?

What could be better?

How has this impacted on how I feel?

Remember:
Give children permission to make mistakes and develop resilience.

Week 6

Reflection:
Perhaps you are finding it difficult to remember what to do next,
maybe it would help if I wrote it down for you.

Child:
Presenting behaviour:

Planned strategies:

What worked?

What could be better?

How has this impacted on how I feel?

Remember:
Every interaction with a child can either erode or enhance their self-esteem.

Week 7

Reflection:
Perhaps it's difficult working in a small group,
maybe it would help if I moved you to sit nearer to me.

Child:
Presenting behaviour:

Planned strategies:

What worked?

What could be better?

How has this impacted on how I feel?

Remember:
Positive, consistent, nurturing relationships are crucial for emotional wellbeing.

Use this space to review the half term – you may want to think about what worked well, what you would do again in the future and any new ideas or things to try.

Section 4

The challenging or demanding child

DOI: 10.4324/9781003379751-7

Focus for the half term

For this half term, we are going to be focusing on and thinking about the children who are more demanding and challenging. These children are desperate to be noticed and they will use many different ways to ensure they achieve this. School staff can spend a lot of time dealing with these children, which can be exhausting and also demoralising, as it can feel like nothing is improving in terms of their behaviour. It may be hard for school staff to remember positive bits of the day as it can feel like the interactions with challenging children are relentless and difficult. Working with these children can be emotionally draining, and often by this stage of the school year, their behaviours are becoming more difficult and exhausting to be around. When school staff are able to think about these children differently, by understanding the possible reasons behind the behaviour, it can feel both liberating and more rewarding for both adults and children. The more curiosity you can have in your approach to these children, the easier it will be to develop empathy, compassion and understanding for them.

Profile checklist

- Their aim is to be noticed and they may go to great lengths to ensure this
- They tend to make their presence known to others and it's very noticeable when they are absent
- Preoccupied with relationships, constantly aware of where the adults are and alert to the availability of others
- Highly dependent and attention seeking
- Overly focused on the relationships with the adults rather than learning
- May talk excessively or be the class clown to maintain the adult's attention
- Finding it hard to follow rules, take responsibility for their behaviour and learn from consequences
- Easily distracted and finding it hard to concentrate on tasks
- Can distract others and try and engage them in being disruptive

How children may present

This child is often the child in your class or school whom all the staff are familiar with; they make themselves known and are often attention seeking and demanding. They need constant attention, are always checking things out and asking questions: 'But why?' They can find it hard to be in the present moment and are constantly wanting to know 'What are we doing next?' They notice everything and often find change very difficult, wanting to know why the change is happening; for example, the class teacher is absent for the day and they keep questioning where they are, why they are not in school, when they will be back, etc. They are vigilant to changes in the classroom, such as wall displays or furniture being moved around, and again will often ask lots of questions about it.

They often have poor impulse control and may shout out, find it hard to sit still and have poor concentration and a short attention span. They may wander around class, find it hard to sit still and fidget with things, especially if the item is connected to an adult, for example a pen lid or a piece of paper that the adult has had. They are very relationship focused and are more interested in what the adults in class are doing and watching them, rather than engaging with their learning. These children often have a strong sense of fairness and injustice and may be preoccupied with looking out for this, particularly in relation to other children. They can be constantly telling tales about other children, as a way of making themselves feel better about who they are: 'Look how bad they are, look how good I am.' They are often in the middle of things that do not involve them and are keen to voice their often-loud opinions about lots of things.

Relationships

They may find peer relationships hard because they can find it difficult to share, listen to others or take turns. They can be bossy and controlling and may try and take over or organise the other children. They may be confused at the adult's response to this behaviour as they think they are being helpful. The other children may avoid them as they can be emotionally immature and unpredictable, so they gravitate towards the adults in school. They can become attached to adults quickly and therefore find the end of the year or separating from adults at any point very difficult. They may lie or blame others as they may be scared of telling the truth or facing the consequences. These children can also find it hard if they think you are cross or unhappy with them or something they have done so may lie to avoid this.

Possible reasons for their behaviour

Most children, especially primary school-age children, want adults to be pleased with them, want to get things right and want to experience the good feelings they have when they are praised for their behaviour. However, for some children, this can feel like an uphill struggle as they attempt to communicate their needs and manage their constant feelings of stress and anxiety. When working with these children, it is essential that school staff try and find out as much as possible about their background (within the constraints of confidentiality) in order to increase their understanding of the child and their behavioural responses. By building up a picture of the child's lives, their relational experiences and their day to day lives, staff are able to gain a better insight into what the child's needs are and attempt to meet them. These children may not have had the opportunity to develop the skills necessary to manage the school day, they may be lacking in resilience, self-esteem and self-regulation and generally have gaps in their emotional and social development.

These children may have experienced unpredictable and inconsistent parenting on a regular basis throughout their lives, including having to be in charge and take care of themselves at an inappropriate age for their development. This can result in them mistrusting the adult relationship and needing to do lots of testing to see what will happen and to work out how the adult will respond to certain situations. They may have few or no boundaries at home and therefore they need to keep checking and testing the rules at school. Whilst this constant checking can be a challenge to manage, especially as it's often done at inappropriate times, for example, in the middle of a lesson, it's often an indication that the child is feeling anxious and worried.

Some of the children who display challenging behaviour in school may have experienced or be experiencing trauma such as physical, emotional or sexual abuse or neglect, witnessing domestic violence, experiencing bereavement or their parent misusing drugs or alcohol or having a mental illness. There may be children in your school who have experienced more than one of these situations. For these children, their experience of the world is very different to children who have experienced consistency and predictability inside their families. When children have experienced trauma, they may not have had their basic needs for safety and security met on a consistent basis and have developed behaviours to help them cope with this. It's important to remember that these behaviours have often been developed as survival strategies and coping mechanisms to enable them to feel safe when they are scared. They are not deliberately being difficult or defiant, although it may appear like this at times.

This child's parent or carer may often be or have been overwhelmed with their own emotional needs and be managing very difficult experiences themselves, which can impact on their ability to be physically and emotionally available for their child. For example, they may be in a violent relationship which can result in them being preoccupied with trying to stay physically safe, and may therefore understandably have limited capacity to fully engage with their child. These children may also have experienced periods of being ignored or met with hostility at times in their lives, resulting in a lack of confidence and low self-esteem which they may have learnt to hide behind a mask of bravado.

For these children, the world can feel unpredictable, unsafe and frightening, if not all the time, then certainly on a regular basis. They may frequently feel scared, worried and anxious and they have developed coping strategies to manage their feelings. They often experience very high levels of anxiety which are increased when there are any changes, even small ones, such as the book corner being moved or the tables being changed. Their anxiety levels may be similar to how school staff feel when they have a lesson observation or Ofsted are in school, but as children, they don't have the same coping strategies as adults; they may not understand or be able to talk about how they feel, and they are unable to understand that it will pass or what the feelings are about as they don't have the same cognitive thought processes as adults. They just experience the feelings, without any skills to understand, express or manage them. Therefore, it is not surprising their feelings are expressed through their behaviour often in a challenging, unpredictable and unregulated way.

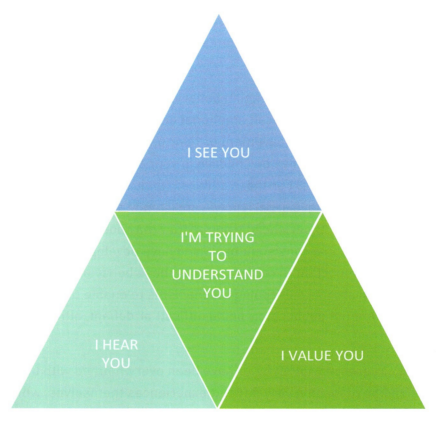

Figure 4.1 Positive messages to the child

Strategies to try

- Remain in charge, be predictable and consistent; this will help them feel safe and secure and reduce their anxiety as they know what to expect.

These children can be challenging, confrontational and argumentative, which can be disorientating and unsettling for staff. The more they experience routine, structure and adults being predictable, the less anxiety and stress they have.

- Ensure the rules and boundaries of both the classroom and the school are explicit, and invest time going through these on a regular basis, checking the child's understanding.

These children may have little or no experience of rules and boundaries outside of school, or they may be constantly changing. It's crucial not to make assumptions about the child's understanding of these and to provide extra support to enable them to follow and remember them.

- If a child is struggling to follow rules, encourage them to choose one rule at a time to work on to achieve success.

This increases the likelihood of a child achieving success and can be a motivator for them to continue practising, rather than feeling overwhelmed and disheartened as they struggle to follow all the rules. A sense of achievement and success can be much harder to achieve for a child who is constantly anxious and they need the experience of small wins to motivate them to continue.

- Try and be reflective rather than reactive. For example, 'I wonder why he's doing that, I wonder how he's feeling.'

This approach encourages the adult to pause and ponder, which may result in an ability to understand and explore what's going on for the child, encouraging a more empathic and less punitive response to the child.

- Use wondering aloud to explore what you think may be happening for them. For example, 'I wonder if you're feeling anxious about the supply teacher coming in, and that's why you're refusing to sit on your chair.'

By wondering aloud, you are giving the message that you are aware that some things are more difficult for them than for other children, which communicates an understanding of their individual needs. It also sends a positive message that you are thinking about them and trying to help them.

- Warn them of changes such as not going outside for P.E. or a member of staff being absent.

Any change may have been negative and unplanned for these children, resulting in them having negative associations with anything being different. When a child is given warning about changes, this enables them to ask questions and try and process what's happening. This approach increases the likelihood of them managing change in a positive and less anxiety provoking way.

- Break tasks into small steps wherever possible. For example, 'I want you to write three sentences, then you can come and show me.'

These children are constantly preoccupied with the adults in school and what they are doing and why. This is particularly true in class and therefore they have very limited capacity to remember more than one piece of information at a time. By breaking tasks down in this way, they are more likely to stay engaged and on task.

- Give them a small object to 'look after' for you whilst you are away from the session.

Although these children are very relationship focused, this will help them to feel a connection to you and help them to remember you are coming back. It can also help them feel more settled and less anxious as they have a sense of you and are able to trust that you will be coming back and that you mean what you say.

- Use their name frequently to remind them that you are thinking about them.

This gives the message 'you matter' to the child and helps them feel valued and important. It can also help them to stay connected to you and helps them to feel important and special, which they may not have experienced on a regular basis before.

- Try to remember that trusting and believing adults may be difficult for the child and incorporate opportunities to remind them of what's happening next. For example, 'I know it's hard to stop when you are doing something you enjoy, but after break you can come back and finish it.'

By doing this on a regular basis, the child will develop trust in what you say and feel less need to challenge you and try to control the situation themselves. The child may still find it difficult to stop immediately, but the reminder that there will be an opportunity to continue later will help them to practise this.

- Create opportunities for regular repetitive jobs. For example, filling water bottles or tidying the book corner.

This provides a break in between other tasks in the day, builds confidence and self-esteem and enables a child to feel helpful and useful. This creates a sense of achievement for a child who may not experience success on a regular basis.

- Give them responsibility for tasks rather than people. For example, giving out cups.

As these children can be domineering and find relationships with other children difficult, the responsibility for a task is more appropriate and is more likely to result in a positive outcome.

- If a child is having regular angry outbursts, provide them with a scribble pad and regular opportunities to use it. For example, provide them with a blank book and encourage them to sit with an adult and show the child how to scribble, explaining how it can be useful to help us get rid of anger. Direct the child to use it if they need it.

This activity provides a positive outlet for their anger and encourages the child to use their anger in a more constructive way. It can also enable them to feel less overwhelmed and consumed by it.

- Accept, acknowledge and validate children's feelings rather than dismissing or discounting them.

These children can often experience their feelings as overwhelming and can find it very hard to manage them. A helpful response to a child who says 'I've got no friends, everyone hates me' could be 'It must be so hard to feel like that', rather than saying, 'That's not true, James likes you.'

- Use frequent, specific praise. For example, 'You were really kind when...'

These children are often not used to receiving positive feedback and may find it hard to believe. Therefore, providing clear and specific feedback on exactly which behaviour they are being praised for enables the child to link up the specific behaviour with the positive feelings they are experiencing, increasing the likelihood of them repeating the behaviour in order to have the good feeling again.

- Involve them in small-group work to develop peer relationships rather than dependency on adults. (For examples, see my group workbooks published by Routledge.)

As relationships with other children are problematic, they need the opportunity to practice doing this in a small and supportive environment. This will develop their skills with peer relationships and encourage them to be less adult focused.

- Return to class at the end of the school day if you have been on PPA (planning, preparation and assessment time, time allocated to teachers to complete duties away from the children) to say goodbye to them and tell them that you will be coming back.

Some children may experience adults coming in and out of their lives on a regular basis, often without being told this is happening or being offered an explanation. If a child knows when you are leaving, that you are returning and when that will be, this reduces their anxiety and fear and frees up space in their brains to engage with other things.

Questions to think about/reflections towards the end of the half term

- How do I feel about children who demonstrate challenging behaviour?
- What responses do these children evoke in me (such as punitive or harsh)?
- Do I ignore some behaviours to avoid confrontation?
- Do I feel more anxious, stressed and agitated when I'm around these children?
- How do I feel when a child with these behaviours is absent?

End-of-half-term summaries

- Children don't always know and may not be able to explain how they feel
- Disruptive and challenging behaviour is often an indicator of anxiety
- Being curious about the reasons behind the behaviour can help a child feel more understood
- Routine and structure can help these children feel safer and more settled
- Invest time and energy into getting to know and understand these children

Week 1

Reflection:
I can see you are looking at that,
maybe you are unsure what to do with it.

Child:
Presenting behaviour:

Planned strategies:

What worked?

What could be better?

How has this impacted on how I feel?

Remember:
Children who show the most challenging behaviour are sometimes the most vulnerable.

Week 2

Reflection:
I can see by your face that you are a bit confused.

Child:
Presenting behaviour:

Planned strategies:

What worked?

What could be better?

How has this impacted on how I feel?

Remember:
When children feel scared and anxious, it can be hard for them to sit still.

Week 3

Reflection:
I can see that you are looking at the...,
maybe you are wondering what it is.

Child:
Presenting behaviour:

Planned strategies:

What worked?

What could be better?

How has this impacted on how I feel?

Remember:
Children that are the hardest to connect with are sometimes the ones who need it the most.

Week 4

Reflection:
I can see by your face that you are unsure about that.

Child:
Presenting behaviour:

Planned strategies:

What worked?

What could be better?

How has this impacted on how I feel?

Remember:
Attention seeking is attention needing.

Week 5

Reflection:
I can see you really want some help with that, and I know it's hard to wait, but I will come over to you when I have finished doing this.

Child:
Presenting behaviour:

Planned strategies:

What worked?

What could be better?

How has this impacted on how I feel?

Remember:
When a child is confrontational they may need help with their anxiety.

Week 6

Reflection:
I can see that you really like having the Blu Tac to hold when you are on the carpet.

Child:
Presenting behaviour:

Planned strategies:

What worked?

What could be better?

How has this impacted on how I feel?

Remember:
Challenging behaviour is a child's way of trying to tell us how they feel.

Week 7

Reflection:
I can see that you are looking angry and
I am wondering why that is.

Child:
Presenting behaviour:

Planned strategies:

What worked?

What could be better?

How has this impacted on how I feel?

Remember:
Trauma impacts on children's learning and wellbeing.

Use this space to review the half term – you may want to think about what worked well, what you would do again in the future and any new ideas or things to try.

Section 5

The invisible child

DOI: 10.4324/9781003379751-8

Focus for the half term

For this half term, we are going to be focusing on and thinking about the children who are sometimes less visible in our class. These children are desperate not to be seen and they will use many different ways to ensure they achieve this. These children have learnt to be wary of adult relationships and they will try to avoid interactions with adults. They can find it overwhelming to ask for help or to even acknowledge this to themselves. They do not draw attention to themselves or like to be the focus of adult attention and will try to avoid this by focusing on their work. Their behaviour may not be causing any immediately observable problems in the classroom. It doesn't usually impact on other children's learning or the teacher's ability to teach the class. They are often missed as their behaviour tends to be more internalised than externalised, and therefore they can initially appear not to be a concern. However, the quiet and withdrawn children in school can sometimes be a bigger concern than the challenging children because they can be easily overlooked as their behaviour has very little impact on the class on a daily basis.

Profile checklist

- Their aim is not to be noticed
- Quiet and withdrawn, fear of failure
- Not trusting others to meet their needs
- Self-reliant and independent, especially for their age
- Reluctant to ask for help when they need it
- Distress is hidden or denied
- Can appear to be ok and settled most of the time
- Fearing intimacy and emotional connection with people
- Resisting help from adults but lack confidence in their own ability
- May appear indifferent to new situations
- Struggling to initiate and respond to relational approaches from others

How children may present

These children are not usually a problem to have in class and can often pass under the radar as they may present as quiet and withdrawn. They are usually compliant, but never or rarely put their hand up, answer questions or initiate asking questions or approaching adults. They may appear to be in their own world and on occasion seem oblivious to what's going on in class or around them. However, they can also be very focused on their work and are very task orientated as a way of avoiding the relationship or drawing attention to themselves. They can appear to be uncaring and may find it hard to show any emotion. Their facial expression may remain the same throughout the day as the events and circumstances around them change; for example, a child may show no remorse when they have hurt another child and appears to have no understanding of other people's feelings, or a child shows no excitement when they hear they have won a prize. It can be very difficult for a child to understand other people's feelings if they have little or no understanding of their own. A child who finds it hard to show feelings may also have learnt to bury their physical pain along with their emotional discomfort. They may have learnt that no matter how much something hurts, it is not safe to make a fuss or ask for help. These children's behaviour is led by self-reliance, and they are usually overly independent, especially for their age, and have learnt that they need to manage everything on their own. They may believe that adults may be cross or ignore them if they ask for help. The prospect of wanting or needing help can be so overwhelming for them that they may miss out on something they enjoy or would like to do, as they are unable to voice their needs.

Relationships

School staff play a vital role in supporting these children and ensuring they feel good about themselves on a daily basis. The quality of the relationship between adults and children is crucial and every interaction can have a positive and meaningful outcome. Everything you say and do can affect children in either a positive or negative way; it can either enhance or erode their self-esteem and sense of self. What we say and how we say it can have a big impact on a child. Our facial expression, body language and tone of voice all have meaning and will be interpreted by the child who is on the receiving end. This is of vital importance for these children, as they are tuned in to adults' every move and are vigilant at trying to translate every movement and gesture, as well as the actual words that are spoken.

When children have had negative experiences of how adults perceive them, they are especially competent at looking for evidence to validate this negative view of themselves. The behaviour of children who are quiet and withdrawn may sometimes be misunderstood and viewed as rude or disrespectful, for example, a child who avoids eye contact and doesn't look at you or respond when you speak to them. It can be beneficial to explore our own feelings when working closely with children who behave in this way; it can be very hard not to have a negative response towards them, even if this is never expressed. These children can be very hard to get to know and it can also be difficult to remember things about them. Although school staff can inevitably end up spending more time with a child who is louder or more attention seeking, it's crucial to make time for these 'invisible' children, even though they can appear to not need or want it.

Possible reasons for their behaviour

A child may find it difficult to show their feelings when they have learnt to internalise rather than externalise their feelings. It can make it more difficult for them to cope at school and to build friendships. These children have often experienced parents or carers who are loud, chaotic and unpredictable, and may also have experienced trauma or witnessed domestic violence. They have learnt that life is very changeable and they may have had to be more self-reliant and independent for their age due to adults not being emotionally or physically available to them. Therefore, they may find it hard to trust an adult and to believe that you mean what you say. This can result in them being more wary, uncertain and cautious, and avoiding the adult relationship.

For these children, the close proximity of adults in the classroom and the constant sense of unpredictability of adult behaviour can feel completely overwhelming. For example, in class the adults are always moving around, approaching children and checking on their work and how they are. This means these children are constantly on high alert and vigilant to any changes or movements from adults, a behaviour which has a huge impact on their ability to feel settled in school, along with impacting on their concentration. They can sometimes appear to be really absorbed in their work, but will always be on the lookout and listening out for adults approaching or potentially asking them to contribute. The early messages these children may have received about being seen and not heard, or learning that they need to try and stay invisible has understandably had a huge impact on them, and may have resulted in them finding it hard to speak out in any situation. The impact of this early experience can create a level of self-sufficiency and independence that can be hard to penetrate and needs to be approached carefully.

It can be useful to reflect on your own feelings as school staff when attempting to interact and build a connection with a child who is quiet or withdrawn. Does it feel like hard work? Do you feel like you are badgering them? Do you feel frustrated and like you want to give up? School staff may feel some or all of these responses as they attempt to develop a relationship with these children. However, the more you can persevere and be aware of your own feelings, the more you are likely to succeed. It can be hard to measure or to see the impact we may have on these children, but there may be small glimmers of change such as a child moving nearer to you or hovering nearby to ask you a question when there are fewer children around. Patience and perseverance are key to making a difference with these children.

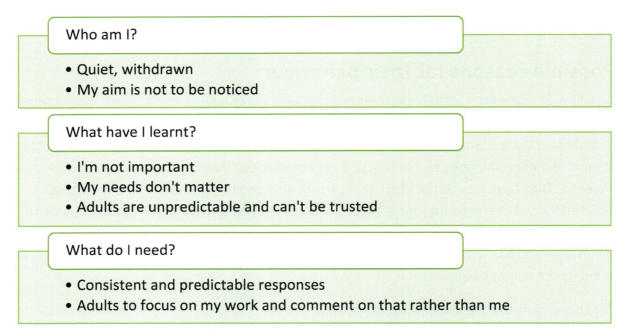

Who am I?

- Quiet, withdrawn
- My aim is not to be noticed

What have I learnt?

- I'm not important
- My needs don't matter
- Adults are unpredictable and can't be trusted

What do I need?

- Consistent and predictable responses
- Adults to focus on my work and comment on that rather than me

Figure 5.1 Understanding the invisible child

Strategies to try

- Don't try and encourage them to approach you or move them to sit nearer to you as this will increase their anxiety, instead, understand their need to focus on the activity or work and have distance from the adult.

This communicates that you understand the child's needs to be more detached and distant, and that you are respecting their need to do this. This gives a positive message to them and can help to reduce their anxiety.

- Support their reliance on the activity and gradually support the child to get help.

As these children have developed self-reliance as a survival strategy, it's important that the move away from this is done very slowly and approached with care and caution.

- Comment on and acknowledge the work they are doing. For example, 'You are working really hard on your maths today.'

By making the work or task the focus, it enables school staff to start gradually building a connection and stay in proximity to the child, without overwhelming them.

- Avoid asking them questions directly in whole class situations or trying to make them look at you and make eye contact.

If a child is unable to contribute or respond to direct questions, it can be helpful to explore what may be going on for the child. Are they so terrified of making a mistake or getting something wrong that they appear to be almost paralysed with fear?

- Try and reflect openly and honestly with yourself about how lack of eye contact makes you feel and explore this.

For some adults, this experience can be viewed as a child being rude or disrespectful; therefore it's important that school staff consider their own feelings about a child who behaves in this way, as this can impact on how they feel about and respond to the child.

- Let them lead the relationship and approach adults when they need to.

This enables the child to feel less fearful and anxious and over time can reduce their need to be on high alert around school staff as they begin to develop a sense of predictability and certainty. This creates the opportunity for them to be less vigilant and therefore feel more relaxed in school.

- Create situations in class on a regular basis where you are modelling asking for help from someone.

This provides the message that 'everyone needs help sometimes' and reinforces that it's ok to ask for help. For example, 'I'm going to ask Mr Chaudhry to help me move the tables later, even adults need help sometimes.'

- Remind them that you can help them if they need it, and offer them the opportunity to indicate that they need help without actually using words. For example, 'It can be hard to ask for help; if you put your hand up or turn this piece of coloured card over, I will know that you need help and come over to you straight away.'

This creates the possibility that a child can tentatively explore trying out a new behaviour without having to use words and speak in front of the whole class. This also enables the child to feel understood and provides the message that school staff are trying to help them by adapting to meet the child's needs.

- Identify and acknowledge aspects of school life that may be difficult. For example, 'I've been thinking about when you fell over outside and didn't tell anyone. Some children find it really hard to tell an adult when they have hurt themselves, but in school, we really care about you and want to make sure you're ok and haven't hurt yourself.'

This provides a strong message that the child is cared for, along with validating their experience of situations that they find difficult. This reinforces that they are important and worth caring for.

- Give structured activities with clear rules and outcomes. For example, problem-solving tasks.

This creates an experience of feeling contained for the child as there are clear boundaries and expectations which the child is better able to work within. Any experience of uncertainty and ambiguity can create fear and anxiety and may result in the child feeling overwhelmed.

- Involve them in paired activities near the adult to help them feel supported in their relationship with adults.

This can enable them to practise interacting with a smaller number of children and provides an opportunity for them to develop their social skills. The more they are able to do this, the more confident they may feel, which increases the likelihood of them participating in larger groups and class over time.

- Give structured activities. For example, building a model or completing a jigsaw.

Tasks like this can provide the child with an opportunity to develop their confidence and self-esteem and achieve a sense of satisfaction by completing a task. The structure of tasks like this provides a clear and concrete experience which the child is more likely to achieve.

- Metaphor can be a useful tool for expression or understanding and is less threatening than more direct communication. For example, stories about houses or castles rather than direct emotional descriptions such as 'feeling safe'.

Talking directly about feelings can be overwhelming for these children as it involves being vulnerable and experiencing trust in the adults. Creating opportunities for them to express feelings in an indirect way through stories provides an emotionally safer way to enable them to do this.

- Avoid mannerisms such as suddenly waving your arms around, even in excitement, as this can cause anxiety and increase stress levels for children who live with unpredictability.

These children have learnt to be vigilant to adult behaviours and can easily misinterpret what is happening and what the adults are doing. Calm and measured movements and explanations about what's happening can really help. For example, 'I'm feeling really excited about our school trip next week.' This enables the child to understand what's happening and to link the movement to the adult behaviour.

- Use a gentle tone of voice and be aware of your facial expressions to help establish a safe relationship for a child who is anxious and scared.

When a child has learnt to read every response an adult makes and to interpret its meaning in a sometimes negative way about themselves, the more experience they have of adults behaving calmly, the less anxious and overwhelmed they feel.

- If a child looks blank or expressionless and finds it hard to show how they are feeling, provide opportunities for them to play 'guess the feeling' using emotion cards with a small group of children and an adult. Identify aspects of facial expressions that enable us to guess how someone is feeling and gradually encourage the group to take turns demonstrating and guessing the emotion they are showing.

When a child is unable to show facial expressions, it can be hard to understand how they feel and they may struggle to read other people's emotions too. This activity can be integrated into the school day or week and can be a relaxed way of developing a child's emotional understanding.

- Remember *all* behaviour is trying to tell us something, so remain curious. For example, 'I wonder why he's looking out of the window, maybe he doesn't know what to do next.'

This is more effective than just reprimanding a child who may find it terrifying to ask for help and is genuinely not sure what to do. This empathic response is more likely to result in the adult understanding and meeting the child's needs.

Questions to think about/reflections towards the end of the half term

- How engaged are all the children in class?
- Do I try to get to know every child in class?
- Do I assume a child who avoids adults is choosing to do so?
- How can I get to know these children better?
- What do I need to be aware of when doing this?

End-of-half-term summaries

- Be aware that if a child is always quiet, it doesn't mean they are ok
- Model asking for help and affirming that everyone needs help
- Accept the child needs to have some distance from school staff and gradually build their trust
- Allow the child to approach you in their own time and at their own pace
- Be patient and accepting of their need to do this

SUPPORT MATERIAL

Week 1

Reflection:
Sometimes it can feel really hard when I'm not in class.

Child:
Presenting behaviour:

Planned strategies:

What worked?

What could be better?

How has this impacted on how I feel?

Remember:
Some children find it scary to ask for help.

Week 2

Reflection:
Sometimes we can feel angry if we get something wrong.

Child:
Presenting behaviour:

Planned strategies:

What worked?

What could be better?

How has this impacted on how I feel?

Remember:
Some children may feel overwhelmed and scared of their feelings.

Week 3

Reflection:
Sometimes it's really frustrating if you've had
your hand up for a long time.

Child:
Presenting behaviour:

Planned strategies:

What worked?

What could be better?

How has this impacted on how I feel?

Remember:
Some children don't physically run off but they may emotionally shut down.

Week 4

Reflection:
Sometimes children can feel sad or upset
when they fall out with their friends.

Child:
Presenting behaviour:

Planned strategies:

What worked?

What could be better?

How has this impacted on how I feel?

Remember:
Some children are preoccupied with what's happening at home.

Week 5

Reflection:
Sometimes children can feel upset if I choose someone else to go first.

Child:
Presenting behaviour:

Planned strategies:

What worked?

What could be better?

How has this impacted on how I feel?

Remember:
Children who are anxious can't access their learning;
reduce their anxiety by helping children feel safe and secure.

Week 6

Reflection:
Sometimes it can be difficult to ask for help;
remember I can help you if you need me to.

Child:
Presenting behaviour:

Planned strategies:

What worked?

What could be better?

How has this impacted on how I feel?

Remember:
Children need help from a caring adult to understand and manage their feelings.

Week 7

Reflection:
Sometimes it's hard when we change our day and do something different; change can be difficult.

Child:
Presenting behaviour:

Planned strategies:

What worked?

What could be better?

How has this impacted on how I feel?

Remember:
Some children are preoccupied with getting through the school day, rather than engaging with it.

Use this space to review the half term – you may want to think about what worked well, what you would do again in the future and any new ideas or things to try.

Section 6

Transition

DOI: 10.4324/9781003379751-9

Focus for the half term

For this half term, we are going to be focusing on and thinking about transition and how to prepare the children to begin separating from you and thinking about moving to a new class after the summer holidays. For some children, this transition period can be very anxiety provoking and stressful, and they will need plenty of support from you to help them with this process. For other children, this creates less anxiety but it is still essential that transition is acknowledged and focused on, with plenty of time allocated to this.

Profile checklist

- Starting to become clingier to you
- Becoming more needy of your time and attention
- Becoming quieter, more withdrawn and in their own world
- Becoming more unregulated, challenging and disruptive in class
- Becoming more detached and distant from you
- May appear indifferent to adults in class
- Behaviour may become more obsessive or controlling of others
- Demonstrating difficulty in managing change
- Beginning to ask about their new class and new teacher and what will happen very early in the half term
- Showing signs of being, anxious, upset or worried whenever transition is mentioned

How children may present

Some of the children in the class may have had previous negative experiences of loss due to bereavement or parents separating. These feelings can be retriggered by the loss of being in your class, which may activate certain behaviours. There may also be children in your class who have experienced being in care or have been adopted or are being fostered. For these children, any relational change can have a massive impact. The impact of these changes may present in different ways, and it's useful to consider that this anxiety can be expressed in both internalising and externalising behaviours. Sometimes a child who has experienced trauma or relational loss may start rejecting school staff with whom they have built a relationship. This can be easier for the child to manage emotionally as they feel they are in charge of the ending. They may start to reject adults before the adult rejects them, which is how they may interpret the end of year transition period.

There may be some other behavioural changes in children. A child may start using a baby voice or develop a sense of helplessness, maybe not being able to do things they have managed easily before. This emotional regression can be an indication that they are feeling emotionally vulnerable and young. A child may also respond to this change happening by developing sudden illnesses such as tummy aches or headaches or finding small cuts on their finger that they show you. This articulating of a child's physical pain may also be an indication that they are in emotional pain and perhaps feel worried, scared or anxious. It can be hard for children to identify how they feel, they may just know that they don't feel right, and this is their way of telling you.

Relationships

Life is a constant struggle and very stressful if we are unable to manage change easily, so it is essential to try and give children a positive experience of managing change when they leave your class at the end of the school year. In order to help children with this, it can be useful if we can demystify the unknown by helping them to name and explore their fears. For some children, relationship loss is a big part of their lives as the significant adults in their lives move away, fall out with their parents or lose interest in them. Some children may have experienced multiple relationship losses in their lives, such as looked after or adopted children who may have lived with several caregivers aside from their parents. Other children may experience adults who are more transient in their lives, for example, a child whose parents are separated and their parents start new relationships, or a child having several new relationships with adults being present then absent from their lives. There may also be children who have experienced bereavements of parents or grandparents and other family members. For these children, it is essential that we try and equip them with the skills they need for survival and success with transition, along with developing a greater understanding of the impact of their experiences.

Possible reasons for their behaviour

School life consists of constant changes for children, but the most difficult change for most children is at the end of the school year as they try to manage an ending and prepare for a new beginning. This end of year change involves managing the unknown of so many new experiences and potentially may include preparing to move to a different building in school, being in a new class upstairs or in a different part of the school building, adjusting to a new class layout along with building new relationships with school staff. All of this understandably creates anxiety for many children as they struggle to manage their feelings about the unknown situations they will be facing when they return to school after the summer holidays.

Some children find any change extremely difficult as it can evoke feelings of loss, anxiety and uncertainty. It is useful, therefore, that children's transitions to new classes are managed with patience and understanding. For a child who has experienced many changes and uncertainties in their life outside of school, the transition to a new class and new teacher can be overwhelming. Be aware that you may not know every child's story of the losses and changes they have experienced in their lives, especially asylum seeker and refugee children and fostered and adopted children, who may have experienced traumatic change and find the transition time in school unbearable and terrifying.

Figure 6.1 Key to a successful transformation

For fostered and adopted children, change may have been a negative and stressful experience, by being removed from their parents and taken to live with people they don't know as well or have a relationship with. Sometimes, this can be in a new area and involve starting at a new school, with this change involving many relationship losses, as well as lots of new experiences to manage. The end of the school year and the losses that can come with that may trigger painful feelings and reminders of the previous losses these children have experienced. It is crucial to be aware of this and to approach these children with empathy and compassion. If you have children in your class who have had these experiences, they need plenty of warning about the end of term approaching and continued repetitive explanations about what will be happening to them. This process needs to be started much earlier in the year than with the rest of the class, preferably after the previous half term or at least six weeks before they will be leaving your class.

The importance of supporting transition

Transition plays a huge part in school life and the importance of allocating time and energy to this cannot be underestimated. If a child has a positive experience of an ending with their class teacher before the summer holiday, this will impact on their ability to return to school and experience a positive beginning with their next teacher. If their end of year experience is not constructive, they may worry about this over the summer and approach the new school year with increased anxiety and trepidation. Ensure you allocate time to thinking and talking about the ending and their year of being in class with you, as well as preparing them for their beginning with their new class teacher.

Sometimes school staff may be concerned that talking about transition too early can cause more anxiety and have a negative impact on children, but the opposite is true. When children are supported by caring adults and given the opportunity to ask questions and share their fears and concerns, this enables them to feel better equipped to deal with the change. It is uncertainty and not knowing that create more anxiety.

The more time that can be allocated to transition before the summer holiday, the easier the transition and settling-in process will be on their return to school. This can result in a decreased level of anxiety for the child, who experiences a sense of predictability and therefore an element of control. When children experience changes as being manageable, it builds resilience and increases the likelihood of them being able to tolerate other life changes in a more positive way.

Strategies to try

• Provide an opportunity for each child to make an 'all about me' poster to be given to their new teacher before their new class transition day. Encourage them to write or draw things they are happy for their new teacher to know about them. For example, 'I love bananas and my favourite colour is red.'

This transitional activity provides both the new class teacher and the child with a starting point to initiate building a connection. It enables the child to pass on information about themselves without having to experience the vulnerability of speaking, which some children may find difficult.

- Create an opportunity to discuss with the whole class some of the experiences you have shared together. For example, 'What do you remember about our school trip or the Christmas performance?' Children can be encouraged to write or draw about this first and to take this home if they wish to and they can be given the choice of you sharing it with the class for them if they don't want to.

This acknowledges the shared experiences and creates a sense of belonging for the class, which is particularly important if the class is going to be mixed with another class next year, or if children are leaving school and going to different schools. It can be interesting to know which experiences each child identifies and to see which are important to them. Giving the children a choice of taking them home enables them to keep the memories if they wish to.

- Create an activity where each child thinks about and draws a poster of the positive things that have happened at school for them this year. This can be given to the next class teacher if they would like them to have it.

This reflective activity enables each child to think about and focus on something positive, which is particularly important for children who may have found the year difficult and those children with whom school staff may have found it more difficult to connect.

- Ensure you spend time with and acknowledge the year and its ending with each child. Although this is time consuming, it can be carried out when the class are doing their poster for the new teacher.

This provides an opportunity for each child and the class teacher to acknowledge any specific events that may be significant for them. For example, 'I remember when you were finding it really hard to understand fractions, but you kept trying and now you can do them easily. I'm very proud of how hard you worked.'

- On the very last day of term, as the children are leaving class for the last time, make time to say a personal goodbye to each child. For example, 'Goodbye Jake, I've really enjoyed having you in my class.'

This individual approach enables each child to feel seen and valued and creates a positive experience of an ending. It's crucial that every child leaves the class for the last time feeling positive about their relationship with the class teacher, so they are not anxious or worried about this over the summer holidays.

- Identify the children who may need extra support with the move and start preparing them for this after the May half term break. Provide weekly walks to the new area and acknowledge any feelings this may evoke in them. For example, 'It can feel a bit difficult moving to another part of the school, but remember there will be lots of people to help you feel settled.'

This provides the message that you know and understand the child and their needs and are thinking about them and putting things in place to help them. The practical aspect of this enables the child to become more familiar with the new area and also creates an opportunity for them to ask any questions they may have. The reminder that the other adults will be there to help them may help to reduce their anxieties about leaving the school staff they are currently with.

- Identify and discuss any significant differences with moving from Key stage one to Key stage two, or from one class to another, such as different playground, change of breaktime or lunchtime.

As there can be a lot of changes to adjust to, it can be useful to identify and discuss these individually. This can help a child to feel less overwhelmed and enable them to process their feelings alongside a caring adult, rather than on their own when they are in their new class and trying to manage lots of other changes at the same time.

- Encourage each child to make a list of the adults in school they can talk to and approach for help and support if they need it

This can be especially helpful for children who find it difficult to ask for help and are overly independent but it can be useful for all children. The task of writing a list and identifying specific school staff that are available for them can help children feel emotionally safer and more settled in school.

- Create opportunities for rehearsing potentially challenging situations, such as getting lost on the way back from the toilet. These can be carried out as role plays with the whole class or with a small group of children.

This opportunity can enable children to face their fears and can help to reduce anxiety. The imagined 'What if...' of situations are usually bigger than the reality, and addressing these beforehand can help dispel these fears.

- Devise social stories of experiences they may have, for example, of class rules being different.

There are often so many differences in the new class that children can easily feel overwhelmed. The identifying and naming of these situations can assist greatly in creating a more positive approach to transition.

- Provide the class with their initial settling in activity to explore how they felt at the start of the year and how they feel now. Use this as an opportunity to explore how well they managed this change.

This provides concrete examples to children that they are resilient and able to manage more than they think. By reflecting with them how well they have dealt with this year and addressed some of their fears, you are providing a template to assist them in facing future changes.

- Acknowledge and keep revisiting the subject of change and ensure the children know they will be able to talk to you even when they are in their new class with another teacher.

Change can be challenging and difficult for children (and adults) to navigate, and can create feelings of fear, anxiety and overwhelm. The more this is talked about in an honest and open way, with feelings being named and acknowledged, the increased likelihood of them managing this. Acknowledging that you will still be available for them if they would like to talk to you can help them to separate from you and attach to their new teacher more easily.

- When they have had their transition time with their new teacher, encourage them to identify and discuss the similarities and differences, along with exploring their feelings about them. For example, 'The tables are set out differently, I'm worried who I will be sitting with.'

By creating this opportunity after their transition time, the children are able to discuss their fears and concerns with an adult they have already built a relationship with. This may encourage them to be more open and honest about their concerns and provides the children with an opportunity to work through them with a trusted adult.

- Provide each child with a memory book for them to have photos of their existing classroom, along with space for staff and children from the class to write a comment or for younger children to draw a picture. This is particularly important for a child or year group who are leaving the school and can be extended to include other school staff and other areas around the school.

This provides children with a lasting memory of their experiences each year and emphasises the importance of marking an ending. The visual memento can provide a reminder of the people and places that have helped them to belong and feel part of their class.

- Create time for each child to make a transition book with photos of their new classroom, new teacher and any other differences, such as a different playground or using a different entrance. Ensure they take these home and encourage parents/carers to look at the books with the children over the summer break.

This provides an opportunity for parents/carers to be involved in supporting transition and enables children to keep a connection with the school over the summer. This will help them transition to their new class more easily.

- Spend time with the teacher who will be having the class after you and create a class portfolio with information on each child to include a photo, some general background information, how they settled into class with you, any relationship issues with children or staff, their likes or dislikes, how they feel about themselves and any strategies that have worked. For example, 'lacks confidence' or 'can find it hard to start working but responds well to adult help starting tasks'.

This approach works well if it can be part of a whole school approach and each teacher receives information about their next class. This detailed handover assists both children and school staff with their initial settling-in period, getting to know each other and speeding up this process.

- After you've had your transition time with your new class, create opportunities to talk to the children in the corridor or in the playground. Invest time getting to know them, commenting on anything you already know about them and acknowledging how much you're looking forward to them being in your class and getting to know them.

This is particularly important for the children that have already been highlighted to you as needing extra relational input. However, all children will feel less worried and more positive about the return to school if they have had an incidental conversation with you. This will benefit children and school staff in September.

Questions to think about/reflections towards the end of the half term

- How am I feeling about this class leaving?
- How can I support myself with this on a practical and emotional level?
- How can I manage my own feelings of loss, sadness and change?
- What is my own experience of endings?
- Do I need extra support at this time of year?
- How can I increase my own self-care and look after my wellbeing?

End-of-half-term summaries

- The end of the school year has a big impact on the beginning of the next one
- Children's behaviour can deteriorate as they try to manage feelings of loss and sadness
- Maintain as much structure, routine and consistency as possible
- Prioritise talking about possible feelings and explaining changes
- Be aware of children's individual experiences, needs and responses to the end of the school year

Week 1

Reflection:
Maybe it feels scary when you have to read out in class; It's hard when we find things difficult.

Child:
Presenting behaviour:

Planned strategies:

What worked?

What could be better?

How has this impacted on how I feel?

Remember:
Some children are managing lots of stress outside of school, which impacts on their ability to concentrate.

Week 2

Reflection:
Maybe it would feel better if I explained that again; it can feel frustrating when we don't know what to do.

Child:
Presenting behaviour:

Planned strategies:

What worked?

What could be better?

How has this impacted on how I feel?

Remember:
Children need praise and acknowledgement of their efforts,
not just their achievements.

Week 3

Reflection:
Maybe I can help if you are unsure
what to do next.

Child:
Presenting behaviour:

Planned strategies:

What worked?

What could be better?

How has this impacted on how I feel?

Remember:
Children who can't self-regulate need patience and support, not punishment.

Week 4

Reflection:
Maybe you can ask someone to play with
you at breaktime.

Child:
Presenting behaviour:

Planned strategies:

What worked?

What could be better?

How has this impacted on how I feel?

Remember:
Children who have experienced trauma may need extra help building relationships.

Week 5

Reflection:
Maybe it's disappointing you didn't get chosen; perhaps you would like to help me do a job instead.

Child:
Presenting behaviour:

Planned strategies:

What worked?

What could be better?

How has this impacted on how I feel?

Remember:
Positive transition sessions and nurturing relational experiences are essential.

Week 6

Reflection:
Maybe you feel worried about going to your new class, change can be difficult.

Child:
Presenting behaviour:

Planned strategies:

What worked?

What could be better?

How has this impacted on how I feel?

Remember:
Some children struggle with the end of term and need extra support.

Week 7

Reflection:
Maybe you feel sad that you are not going to be in my class anymore, but I will see you around school and you can come and talk to me.

Child:
Presenting behaviour:

Planned strategies:

What worked?

What could be better?

How has this impacted on how I feel?

Remember:
Children's feelings about moving class and leaving their teacher must be acknowledged and validated.

Use this space to review the half term – you may want to think about what worked well, what you would do again in the future and any new ideas or things to try.

Conclusion

I hope you have enjoyed using this book and that it has had a positive impact on you and the children you work with. I frequently see school staff doing amazing work with children in our schools. I see calm and nurturing responses to challenging behaviour, and patience and understanding when trying to meet children's emotional needs. It takes empathy, compassion, patience and an enormous amount of understanding to stay child focused and determined to make a difference. Relationships matter and it's never too late to make a difference to a child. School staff need to be as physically present, emotionally available, responsive and caring as they can be. Schools have a crucial role to play in developing positive mental health and wellbeing in children, and in the prevention of further difficulties in adult life.

The weekly reflections and half term focus create an ideal and easy way to experiment with responding differently, along with providing opportunities for children to experience new ways of having their feelings acknowledged and validated. This in turn supports children in understanding, expressing and managing their feelings. As adults, we may try to protect children from experiencing sadness, hurt and upset, but these are part of life along with happiness, joy and excitement. When we are able to support children to understand, articulate and experience all feelings, rather than only some feelings, we are creating a solid foundation for their emotional and mental wellbeing.

Throughout this book, I have been encouraging school staff to try different strategies to respond to children's behaviour. It can be easy in life to keep doing things the way we've always done them and harder to be brave enough to experiment with another way. However, the significant relationships between school staff and children that can occur in school settings enable both children and staff to experiment with this concept. The more that school staff can get to know and understand the children in their care, the more they will be able to develop appropriate responses to their behaviour and meet the child's needs.

Every child deserves to be happy, safe and settled in school, be equipped with the skills to build friendships, the confidence to do well and the opportunity to reach their full potential. Children need the opportunity to feel they belong, are worthwhile, have something to offer and can make a contribution to the world. Children need to feel they have a purpose in the same way as adults do.

DOI: 10.4324/9781003379751-10

Don't underestimate the crucial role you can play in changing a child's experience of life and relationships. It may not be noticeable immediately or measurable straight away, but you never know what seeds you have planted or when they will grow. Many adults are able to remember a teacher who has had a positive impact on them and can recall what that teacher did and how it made them feel. All school staff have a responsibility to invest time, thought, energy and commitment into exploring how they can contribute to and enhance children's emotional wellbeing on a daily basis. Every member of school staff has a role to play in helping children reach their full potential. You have to believe you can make a difference and start making it today.

The impact that positive and nurturing educational experiences can have on children is invaluable. There are endless possibilities throughout the school day to introduce emotional vocabulary, provide children with skills and opportunities to express their feelings and produce experiences that enable them to learn about their emotional health and wellbeing, along with creating situations to enable children to feel good about themselves.

Schools are in an ideal position to provide children with positive and nurturing relationship experiences which can provide children with an alternative relational template to the one they may have within their families. When we meet children's emotional and social needs, we remove the barriers that create blockages and enable them to learn.

I decided to include the example of 'Think of Jim' as I use it frequently when I deliver training and it always has a powerful impact on the school staff that hear it. I suggest you read it slowly and try to absorb it.

From 0 - 10 years

- Jim hears what a bad person he is at home every day
- His behaviour at school is challenging and disruptive
- The school staff find it hard to manage his behaviour and unconsciously reinforce the messages he has received at home that he is a bad person

From 10 - 20 years

- Jim struggles with friendships and relationships
- He is often in trouble with the police

From 20 - 30 years

- Jim criticises and struggles to manage his own children's behaviour and to have a good relationship with them

From 30 - 40 years

- Jim's kids don't want to see him
- He is drinking heavily to drown out the internal voice that keeps telling him he is a bad person

Imagine

- If at age 5 Jim had been a pupil at your school

Imagine

- If he had been flooded with messages that had told him he was a good person

Imagine

- If he had experienced the school staff showing him he was a worthwhile person who had good qualities to share with the world

Imagine

- If he had taken that confidence and self-esteem and positive sense of himself when he left school

Imagine

- What his life could have been like at age 20, 30 or 40

Imagine

- If he had been lucky enough to come to your school

Figure 7.1 Think of Jim

Index

Note: Page numbers in *italics* reference figures.